CONTEN

*This book is dedicated to the seekers of health
and to those who help them find it.*

ACKNOWLEDGEMENTS

I should like to express my gratitude to Dr Andrea Kingston for her valuable input and the enlightened way she dealt with a number of apparent contradictions between orthodox medicine and complementary therapies; to nutritionist Angela Dowden for offering many pertinent suggestions; to Sato Liu of the Natural Medicines Society for her assistance in providing contacts and arranging interviews with practitioners; and to my agent Susan Mears for her encouragement and practical help.

This book could not possibly have been written without the co-operation of the following practitioners who have so willingly endured my interruptions: aromatherapy – Christine Wildwood; naturopathy – Jan De Vries; homoeopathy – Michael Thompson and Beth MacEoin; reflexology – Pauline Wills; and anthroposophical medicine – Dr Maurice Orange.

I must thank my daughter Sukaina for giving her time during vacation from university for wading through research papers and books and extracting relevant information. Last but not least, I wish to thank my wife Latifa whose gentle care and concern, not to mention long hours typing the manuscript, enabled me to complete this book.

Foreword To The Series

from the Natural Medicines Society

When we visit our doctor's surgery and are given a diagnosis, we often receive a prescription at the same time. More people than ever are now aware that there may be complementary treatments available and would like to explore the possibilities, but do not know which kind of treatment would be most useful for their problem.

There are books on just about every treatment available, but few which start from this standpoint: the patient interested in knowing the options for treating their particular condition – which treatment is available or useful, what the treatment involves, or what to expect when consulting the practitioner.

The Headway Healthwise series will provide the answers for those wishing to consider what treatment is available, once the doctor has diagnosed their condition. Each book will cover both the orthodox and complementary approaches. Although patients are naturally most interested in relieving their immediate symptoms, the books show how complementary treatment goes much deeper; underlying causes are explored and the patient is treated as a whole.

It is important to stress that it is not the intention of this series to replace the expertise of the doctors and practitioners, nor to encourage self-treatment, but to show the options available to the patient.

As the consumer charity working for freedom of choice in medicine, the Natural Medicines Society welcomes the Headway Healthwise series. Although the Natural Medicines Society does not recommend people who are taking prescribed orthodox medicines to stop doing so, our aim is to introduce them to complementary forms of treatment. We believe the orthodox system of medicine is often best used as a last, not first, resort when other, gentler, methods fail or are inappropriate.

Giving patients the information to make their choice is the purpose of this series. With the increasing use of complementary medicine within the NHS, knowing the complementary options is vital both to the patients and to their doctors in the search for better health care.

Foreword To The Book

Admitting that you have a dependency or addiction is difficult. It is also the first, essential step towards improving your situation. If you are looking at this book, or buying it, as part of admitting that you, or someone close to you, has a dependency problem, you are already making progress.

Dependency, whether on tobacco, alcohol, excess food or other substances, is one of the most shadowy areas of ill health. The difficulty of admitting it signals society's confused attitude; how much is it the sufferer's 'own fault', or character weakness, how much an effect of inherited personality that the sufferer cannot control, how much a physical illness? How much is the sufferer a straightforward victim, due to youthful exposure to our society's historic acceptance of some legal but addictive habits?

Many health problems carry a similar mixture of influences, but in dependency they are more obvious. So it is far harder to seek medical help for a compulsive eating problem, for example, than for high blood pressure, although in theory most cases of high blood pressure are equally self-caused.

This makes *Alcohol, Smoking, Tranquillisers* especially useful in presenting practical ideas for treating dependency from the whole spectrum of medical approaches, including the role of self-help. Courage! A useful starting point is to realise that all humans have some dependencies: our daily habits. Don't blame yourself and don't imagine that 'normal people' are free of dependency: the aim is to find a level and a set of habits that improve, not reduce, the quality of life. Many people succeed.

Miriam Polunin
Author and Health Writer,
Chairman of the Natural Medicines Society

PREFACE

Headway Healthwise is a concise new series which takes the original approach of looking at common ailments and describing how they may be treated using complementary therapies. The aim of the series is not to replace the orthodox medical approach but to give readers an overview of how they may be helped by consulting complementary practitioners.

Once a condition has been diagonised by a GP, those wishing to avail themselves of other forms of treatment will find this book particularly useful. The intention of this series is not to recommend people taking prescribed orthodox medicines to stop taking these. It is to introduce them to alternative and complementary forms of treatment which may enable them reduce the amount of orthodox prescriptions, at the very least, and, in many cases, do away with their need altogether.

We have attempted to present the information in a style that is clear and easy to read. The central approach is to look at addiction from different perspectives by providing you with descriptions of several complementary therapies. While cautioning against self-medication, the book has been written to encourage you to take charge of your own health by making an informed choice of therapy. It shows how and why orthodox medicine – a life-saving and useful system of medicine – should be used as a last resort when other more natural methods fail, rather than the first recourse.

An overview of addiction in the opening chapter is followed by a chapter on the kind of treatment to expect from your GP. The second chapter deals with such factors as lifestyle, diet and nutrition in the management of the disorder. Later chapters look at complementary approaches to the subject.

The one common factor that underpins all the alternative or complementary therapeutic techniques described in this book is the belief in the healing power of the body. Practitioners recognise that the body possesses an inherent ability to cure itself. This gives a clear message to the patient of his/her role in the healing process – that of the mind willing the body to heal itself.

At first sight this may appear to challenge the approach of orthodox medicine, in which the therapeutic objective is to cure the

diseased part of the body. The patient has no role to play except dutifully to take the medicine. The concept of a white-coated god who possesses the magic pill to cure is the result of fear combined with a lack of understanding of the nature of disease and, more so, that of health.

This book is an attempt to dispel myths and to bring about a greater understanding of the issues relating to health and healing, which go beyond the realms of simple anatomy and biology. The recognition that orthodox medicine and complementary therapies need not be mutually exclusive, as both have a role to play, can go a long way towards promoting the integrated medicine of the twenty-first century.

Hasnain Walji
Milton Keynes
January, 1994

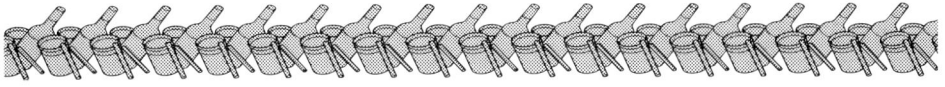

Note: Any information given in this book is not intended to be taken as a replacement for medical advice. Any person with a condition requiring medical attention should consult a medical professional.

Throughout the book you will find some words in italics. If these are not immediately explained, you will find the explanation in the glossary.

OVERVIEW: DO NOT SURRENDER

It starts off innocently enough: pleasure derived from a drink after work with colleagues; a tough work-out at the gym; a video game which engages your mind; a 'joint' passed to you at a party. Usually, if things are stable in other areas of life, the pleasure remains simply that – a pleasure. But sometimes the pleasure becomes a necessity and what was once a take-it-or-leave-it option develops into an integral part of each day. Doing without is unthinkable and instils, among other things, anxiety and irritability. The former source of pleasure becomes the master, no longer the servant.

The word 'addiction' comes from the Latin *addicare*, meaning 'to surrender'. Addiction is neither a modern nor Western phenomenon. The Victorians were prey to the powerful drugs laudanum, opium and morphine, and European artists and poets of the last century enhanced their creativity, so they believed, by experimenting with various hallucinogenic drugs. The Druids enhanced their religious practices through the mind-altering effects of wild mushrooms. Present-day Nigerians love their kola nut (the nut of the coca tree) the Indians their beetle nut and Somalis their marungi (a type of leaf).

Research shows that addictions in their various guises are on the increase. In the UK, 11.6 million people drink too much alcohol; 500,000 are addicted to *tranquillisers* (calming drugs); there are more than double the drug addicts now as there were in 1971 – and these figures reflect only the known cases. But why is addiction on the increase?

The availability of harmful substances plays a large part: although smoking is increasingly disallowed in public places and is, in fact, on a downturn; *marijuana* (also known as *cannabis* – the leaves and flowers of the hemp plant) is gaining social acceptance; alcohol is freely obtainable and although it has always been a part of society, we can now buy it with our cornflakes from the supermarket; video games are a part of life for schoolchildren; and although advertising is stripping the glamour from the highly addictive narcotic, *heroin*, the use of *cocaine* (derived from coca leaves or synthesised) is on the

increase. This brings us to consider the nature of addictive pursuits and the profile of an addict. Who are addicts, and why do they become addicted?

What Is Addictive?

Substance addiction is easily recognised – alcohol, tranquillisers, *caffeine* (the addictive substance found in tea and coffee), drugs, sugar and *nicotine* (the addictive substance found in tobacco) are the commonest physically addictive substances. But there is more to addiction than the body craving for a particular substance. The mind also has a major role to play and addictions often have psychological implications. For example, people can be addicted to gambling and we are hearing more about children's addiction to video games; these addictions are mental rather than physical.

This book is mainly about substance addiction, and in a moment we will look at some common substances which lead to addiction.

How Do We Get Addicted?

Need is the root of all addiction. There can be many reasons why the need arises – often following attempts to fill a void or to escape from a problem: a void left by the death of someone close, or divorce, or redundancy or simply boredom; financial problems, work pressure, relationship difficulties, personal dissatisfaction or low self-esteem. Pleasure, of course, is another cause of addiction or dependency.

A number of addictions are said to be stress-related. After a busy morning a cup of tea or coffee almost appears a godsend. *Caffeine* or *tannins* (substances found in tea and coffee) are *stimulants* which perk us up. Sugar causes an increase in blood sugar levels which increases energy levels, albeit for a short time only. Alcohol helps us to relax, releasing anxiety, inhibitions and increasing self-confidence; *hard* (highly addictive) drugs or cigarettes have the same effect. The effects of a trauma of any type can be dulled temporarily by taking tranquillisers, and if used correctly, tranquillisers can aid in the healing process.

When life becomes dull and unsatisfying and we do not know how to improve our general situation, a lift in spirits can reverse a negative outlook and provide the spur to take action to change the dreary or niggling aspects of life. Some people achieve this through

the intellectual stimulation from conversation with others, or reading, going to the theatre, listening to music or perhaps visualisation or meditation. A quicker and less demanding route is to take a pill or have a drink of alcohol.

Addictions usually begin innocuously from a need for a temporary escape from the problems of everyday life. Unfortunately, the temporary escape can become infinitely preferable to workaday reality and its problems. Avoiding the issue buys time to come up with a solution or, more often than not, to avoid the necessity for change and the will to implement it.

But it is not all doom and gloom: although it may not have seemed so at the time, the decision to take an escape route is a decision – a decision to avoid reality. Stopping a habit is simply a reversal of that decision.

Alcohol

Alcohol may appear to be a pleasure but, taken in excess, is a curse. Advertising campaigns concentrate on the pleasure alcohol gives us: it is a way of socialising, a means of celebrating, and its effects can make us relaxed and trouble-free. The price of over-indulgence is a hangover the next morning. But that is only the start.

Our bodies are sophisticated mechanisms, and pain is the body's way of warning us that something is not right and that we should look to set it right. So the hangover symptoms – headache, thirst, dizziness and nausea – occur because the body's systems have been disturbed. The body can deal with the occasional hangover and recover from it. Heavy drinking over a long period of time is another matter, causing long-term damage.

For a start, the liver is overburdened with alcohol as it tries to convert the alcohol into energy. An impaired liver function can bring an imbalance to the body generally; 10 to 30% of heavy drinkers go on to develop *cirrhosis,* which deforms the liver due to massive scarring and dead liver tissue, which can be fatal. Alcoholic *hepatitis* (inflammation of the liver)and *jaundice* (a disease which causes yellowness of the skin) due to liver failure are also consequences of heavy drinking. The brain is affected by heavy drinking since brain cells are literally destroyed by alcohol. Impaired brain function leads to depression, anxiety, lapse of memory – not to mention the more serious brain disorders of dementia, epilepsy and hallucinations. The pancreas may become inflamed and this lowers

blood sugar levels so that the heavy drinker feels tired and drained. Disturbance in the *metabolic processes* (the chemical processes in the body) leads to malnutrition, as damage to the digestive tract interferes with the body's ability to absorb nutrients. As alcoholics consume more alcohol than food, there are deficiencies in some essential nutrients, in particular the B vitamins. Cell regeneration is affected, as is the immune system.

Alcoholics are much more prone to heart attacks and abnormal heart rhythms because the strength and contraction of the heart muscle is affected by alcohol. Circulation is damaged, showing itself by numbness or tingling in the fingers. Impaired blood circulation increases the risk of a *stroke* (a sudden attack that causes unconsciousness and is often followed by paralysis or loss of feeling in the body).

Even very modest amounts of alcohol can affect the reproductive system. As the male hormone *testosterone* is eliminated faster and less is produced, the male heavy drinker often experiences a lessened *libido* (sexual drive) and potency, and sperm production is lowered. Female heavy drinkers may suffer irregular periods and breast shrinkage and are more prone to develop cancer. It is not just an old wives' tale that women cannot drink as much as men: a smaller liver means smaller absorption of alcohol, which is why no woman should try to match or beat a man when it comes to drinking. Most of us have heard of the dangers of drinking while pregnant: alcohol passes through the umbilical cord directly to the *foetus* (developing baby). Babies born of alcoholic mothers may be impaired mentally and physically.

Coming off alcohol is not easy, perhaps all the more so since we are constantly surrounded by its easy availability and its role in our social lives. But support, such as Alcoholics Anonymous groups, is available to the alcoholic who decides to give up.

Caffeine

Caffeine is present in coffee and tea, our most familiar daily drinks. Tea and coffee provide a welcome lift during a busy day and are also sociable drinks. A problem arises if you begin to rely on coffee or tea to keep going. Since caffeine raises blood sugar levels, it gives you a boost when your energy levels are flagging. Unfortunately, when your blood sugar levels return to their norm, your body feels tired again and you look to another cup to keep you going.

Since the oils in coffee can irritate the gut, too much strong coffee can cause digestion problems and an upset stomach. Caffeine increases the heart rate and blood pressure, so people with *hypertension* (abnormally high blood pressure) should restrict their caffeine intake. Many people are aware that too much coffee can bring on a migraine – not surprising since caffeine has the effect of widening the blood vessels which causes pain.

In addition, heavy caffeine drinkers have a higher risk of heart disease, and pregnant women should be warned that there is a link between caffeine consumption and low birth-weight.

As caffeine addiction arises out of a need to boost flagging energy levels and maintain or increase concentration, it is advisable to remove the need for caffeine, and then to build up the body's energy levels in other ways. Herbal teas and decaffeinated coffee are useful substitutes.

Nicotine

Nicotine use is generally decreasing in this country, thanks to the well-publicised effects of smoking, but unfortunately it is still increasing among teenage girls.

But what are the well-publicised health risks of smoking? Each puff of cigarette smoke releases thousands of different chemical compounds, some of which are *carcinogens* (substances which produce cancer). Tar coats the lungs, nicotine cuts down blood oxygen. Nicotine, the addictive substance in smoking, at first stresses the body by constricting blood vessels, then calms it by stopping the flow of the chemical *adrenaline* and the transmission of nerve impulses along the muscles.

Smokers enjoy cigarettes for a number of reasons: one is the tranquillising effect smoking brings; smoking enhances concentration and also suppresses the appetite. Smoking is a useful social prop for the insecure. Earlier this century it held a glamourous appeal; nowadays we understand the far-reaching and terrible effects that nicotine has on health – both on the smoker's health and on the health of passive smokers – who only inhale other people's smoke, but do not smoke themselves. The unborn child can suffer from a mother's smoking habit and nicotine also finds its way into breast milk.

Because there are so many reasons for smoking, it is extremely difficult for some people to give up, but many people have

succeeded and have found complementary medicine particularly
helpful in doing so.

Sugar

The human body does not need sugar. We consume it for pleasure
in sweets, cakes and biscuits, and unthinkingly in breakfast cereals,
bread and even hamburgers. It does not take much to overload the
system with sugar and with it create a see-saw of love–hate addiction
to the substance.

Natural sugar, when it is still part of sugar beet or sugar cane, is
good for us. The sugar which we consume has been refined beyond
recognition and stripped of its nutrients. We have all felt the effects
of an upsurge in energy after eating a chocolate bar and the
tiredness and desire for more, which follows soon after. This is
because on eating sugar the level of sugar in our blood rises, in
response to which the pancreas releases the chemical *insulin* to
lower the blood sugar to normal. If this happens in large amounts
and on a frequent basis the pancreas releases ever more insulin in
an attempt to keep up with the influx of sugar until eventually it may
malfunction and the body reacts unfavourably to any sugar at all,
resulting in the disease *diabetes*. As well as affecting energy levels,
sugar feeds yeast, with the result that the fungus *Candida albicans* is
common among high consumers of sugar. That in itself affects the
body in many ways – mood swings, constipation or diarrhoea,
lethargy, acne, migraine, menstrual problems. Candida is extremely
unpleasant and difficult to be rid of once it takes hold.

Sugar, of course, rots teeth and makes it easy to put on weight.
The irony is that high consumers of sugar are more than likely
unaware of the root of their problems, and continue to indulge in
sugary confections to cheer themselves up.

Overcoming the sugar habit is not as easy as you might think. For
one thing, sugar addiction is not yet widely recognised among the
medical profession. Re-educated eating habits and some relevant
complementary medicine provide the answer.

Tranquillisers

Before the late 1970s it was thought that drugs should be used to
cure anything and everything. It was not understood that the body
produces symptoms in response to disease or infection as part of its

way of curing itself. The medical thinking at the time was that if you cured the symptom, you cured the patient. It was also thought that the patient should be numbed from any pain or discomfort. Consequently pills were prescribed freely and without much concern for their possible addictive nature.

There are different groups of drugs that act on the central nervous system, dampening awareness and blurring sensitivity. In one group are *barbiturates,* which are general central depressant drugs, acting on all of the brain's activities and hence affecting mind and body. The second group acts more specifically on parts of the brain which affect our levels of anxiety but nothing else: in this group are the *benzodiazepines* (Valium, Librium and Ativan are in this group). There is a third class of drugs called *beta-blockers* which reduce the physical effects of anxiety. This last group carries the least risk of addiction; the second group, depending on the drug, carries a reasonable to moderately high risk of dependence; while the first group, no longer used as tranquillisers (see Chapter 2) into which barbiturates fall, carries a low to very high likelihood of dependence, depending again on the type of drug.

Withdrawal symptoms can be minimised to a few days or a few weeks (how long the drugs have been taken and how high the dosage are important factors) if withdrawal is undertaken in stages: it is very important not to decide yourself how to come off tranquillisers but to work out a withdrawal plan with your practitioner. Nowadays many GPs encourage the patient to set the pace of withdrawal and to remain in control of the plan. Typically, you will be given guidelines for cutting down, for example reducing by 10 to 20 mg per week – it is up to you if it is 10 mg or 12 mg or 20 mg. The lessons of the last few decades have also changed the way in which many GPs prescribe tranquillisers: a short course is usually offered and an eye kept open for any signs of dependency.

Food

You may be surprised to see food considered in this book as an addiction but it is a very real problem. There are different types of food addiction. One is the addiction to food itself; here the actual food is irrelevant. Any type of food relieves anxiety, boredom and frustration and eating is for eating's sake. The problems here are psychological, and specialised treatment should be sought – your GP will be able to advise you.

In contrast, particular foods, such as sugar and xanthine-bearing foods (e.g. coffee and chocolate), may be addictive. This type of addiction arises from an unbalanced diet which can be redressed by attention to nutrition. The *Hay Diet*, for example, states that our traditional concept of a 'proper meal' being 'meat and two veg' is one of the most difficult food combinations for the body to digest. The Hay Diet advises avoidance of a mixture of food types, typically carbohydrates with meat followed by a sweet dessert, and prescribes meals where the foods are of the same type of nutrient and are therefore easier for the body to digest.

Then there are the food addictions which arise because of the psychologically addictive nature of the foods, for example, junk foods, processed foods, and, of course, chocolate and sugar. It is useful to remember that healthy foods, that is, fruit, vegetables, fish, wholemeal products, etc., cannot by themselves lead to addiction since they are well balanced and do not upset the body's systems. It is the chemically laden, unhealthy foods which can create addictions. Correct diet will remedy this food problem.

Heroin

So far we have explored substances which are easily available, or fairly easily available, and which are legal. But, of course, hard drugs, illegal drugs, are also addictive and we briefly mention them here.

When we speak of addiction, heroin is the drug which often comes to mind, and with good reason. A derivative of opium, just one injection can lead to addiction.

Physically, heroin slows down the body's functions, so that heartbeat, muscles and breathing are relaxed and mental and physical pain are numbed; as an anaesthetic, heroin is a useful medical drug. The side-effects, however, include dizziness, vomiting, malnutrition, muscle-wasting and impairment of the immune system. Overdose can lead to death simply because all the body's functions have been slowed down to such an extent that everything just stops.

Of course, a heroin addict is not concerned with the danger of the drug because to him/her, it leads to an experience which nothing else can equal. Addiction is caused in part by the drug's powerful chemicals which override the body's *endorphins* (chemicals in the brain which give a sense of happiness). Heroin affects the

brain so that eventually it cannot produce endorphins: happiness, or any sense of well-being, is therefore impossible naturally and becomes completely dependent upon heroin.

The effects of heroin are a major factor in its mental addictive nature. The heightened effect on the physical senses which heroin induces will either fascinate or disturb the drug user, and then addiction is guaranteed. The substance takes over and the body and mind surrender to it. Will-power, the conviction that stopping is easy, and the resolve to abstain, fade with the drug's hallucinatory effects.

Addiction to heroin is consequently more psychological than most other substances which, when coupled with its effect on the body, makes it a dangerous drug indeed. However, many people with the will to kick heroin have succeeded in doing so, not by replacing one drug with another but by using complementary medicine and therapies, as we shall describe in later chapters.

Cocaine

Cocaine is obtained from the leaves of the coca plant. In South America, the Incas revered coca and thought it a gift from god. For centuries coca was used legally in this country by poets and writers until opinion began to change during the late nineteenth century. Coca became artificially reproduced as cocaine and used in medicine.

Cocaine inspires feelings of supreme self-confidence and mental well-being, and makes the user very active. The 'high' is short term, however, and is followed by a 'downer' of depression, bad temper and negative outlook. Cocaine has an immediate effect on the central nervous system and releases stress hormones so that blood pressure, heartbeat and body temperature rise. Since cocaine is often *snorted* (inhaled through the nose), long-term use damages and destroys the membrane separating the nostrils. Blocked *sinuses* (cavities in the skull), nosebleeds and other complaints are common in long-term users of cocaine. Hallucinations, *paranoia* (unfounded fear or suspicion), exhaustion and muscle weakness and, with prolonged usage, *seizures* (sudden attacks of a disease, such as epileptic convulsions) and brain damage are all effects of cocaine addiction.

So why is use of this drug on the increase?– for the feeling of confidence it inspires and the physical energy it creates. (Several

pop stars and people in the entertainment world have been renowned users of this dangerous drug, which gives it a spurious glamour.)

Withdrawal affects both the body and mind, the latter being more difficult to control. If addicts begin using cocaine for the feeling of self-confidence it induces, they need to find other means of boosting their self-esteem before they give up the drug itself. For many ex-addicts, the fact that they have kicked their addiction proves to them that they are capable of more than they perhaps thought.

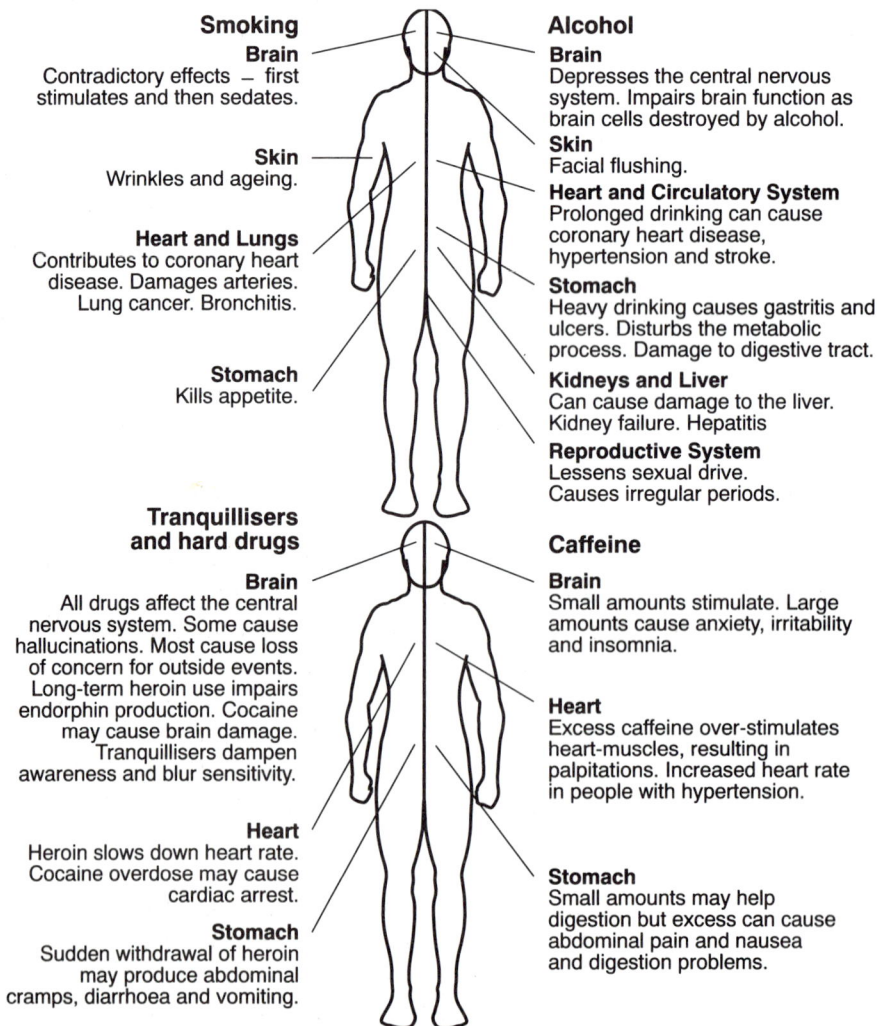

Smoking

Brain
Contradictory effects – first stimulates and then sedates.

Skin
Wrinkles and ageing.

Heart and Lungs
Contributes to coronary heart disease. Damages arteries. Lung cancer. Bronchitis.

Stomach
Kills appetite.

Alcohol

Brain
Depresses the central nervous system. Impairs brain function as brain cells destroyed by alcohol.

Skin
Facial flushing.

Heart and Circulatory System
Prolonged drinking can cause coronary heart disease, hypertension and stroke.

Stomach
Heavy drinking causes gastritis and ulcers. Disturbs the metabolic process. Damage to digestive tract.

Kidneys and Liver
Can cause damage to the liver. Kidney failure. Hepatitis

Reproductive System
Lessens sexual drive. Causes irregular periods.

Tranquillisers and hard drugs

Brain
All drugs affect the central nervous system. Some cause hallucinations. Most cause loss of concern for outside events. Long-term heroin use impairs endorphin production. Cocaine may cause brain damage. Tranquillisers dampen awareness and blur sensitivity.

Heart
Heroin slows down heart rate. Cocaine overdose may cause cardiac arrest.

Stomach
Sudden withdrawal of heroin may produce abdominal cramps, diarrhoea and vomiting.

Caffeine

Brain
Small amounts stimulate. Large amounts cause anxiety, irritability and insomnia.

Heart
Excess caffeine over-stimulates heart-muscles, resulting in palpitations. Increased heart rate in people with hypertension.

Stomach
Small amounts may help digestion but excess can cause abdominal pain and nausea and digestion problems.

Some physical effects of addictions

Giving Up The Addiction

Just as an addiction takes a while to take hold, so you will have to be patient to be free of the craving, as it may take your body quite a long time to eliminate the substances and the accumulated toxins and for your emotions to stabilise. The first step is to decide to give up an addiction and to stay off the addictive substance. The second step is to accept that it is not going to be easy.

We all start a new diet with the greatest of resolve. But halfway through many of us ask ourselves why we are bothering with it when it is so unpleasant and uncomfortable. Kicking an addiction is much more difficult, but with determination can be achieved. Doubts about continuing must be resolved with the thought that you owe it to yourself, and the reward of living a life free of the addiction will be well worth all the short-term struggles.

All forms of addiction are harmful for the damage they do to the body itself and for the emotional and psychological dependence they create in the addict. Kicking any habit requires patient, gentle understanding from your practitioner, the support of your family and friends and the will to stop on your part. The addiction did not take hold in a day, and you cannot rush the process of coming off your addiction. Expect the occasional relapse but do not use a relapse as an excuse to give up your withdrawal plan. Instead, regard it as part of the normal process of giving up dependency.

Your GP could be your first port of call – particularly if your addiction is severe or life-threatening (see Chapter 2). However, a gradual withdrawal is best advised since that places the least strain and stress both on your mind and your body. Herbal and homoeopathic medicines (see Chapters 4 and 5), appropriately prescribed, are gentle, gradual and free from side-effects. Complementary therapies, such as aromatherapy, acupuncture, and anthroposophical medicine (see Chapters 6 to 8), also offer largely drug-free solutions to break the addictive chain, and make sure you stay off your addiction for good. Almost all complementary therapies aim to treat you holistically – your body, mind and spirit – to get to the root of the addiction. Most practitioners will also focus on nutrition (see Chapter 3) as an essential element for the management of a withdrawal programme. Its impact on health and and well-being cannot be overemphasised.

A lot of effort on your part is needed: it is no use going to a medical professional or therapist and saying 'Here's my body – get

rid of my addiction while I get on with the rest of my life as before'. *It is you who has to play the leading role.* Whatever your choice of therapy, the key words are *self-discipline, will-power* and an *increased self-esteem.* Whether you are dependent on alcohol, nicotine, caffeine, sugar, Valium or heroin, the principles are the same: if you want to give it up, you can!

Useful Addresses

Alcoholics Anonymous, PO Box 1, Stonebow House, York YO1 2NJ, Telephone: 0904 644026, is a voluntary, worldwide organisation for men and women from all walks of life who meet together in local groups.

Alcohol Concern, Waterbridge House, 32–36 Loman Street, London SE1 OEE, Telephone: 071-928 7377, refers people to local services, usually one-to-one counselling.

ASH (Action on Smoking and Health), 109 Gloucester Place, London W1H 3PH, Telephone: 071-935 3519, aims to alert the public to the dangers of smoking, but does not offer counselling.

Eating Disorders Association, Sackville Place, 44 Magdalen Street, Norwich, Norfolk NR3 1JU, Helpline Telephone: 0603 621414, offers information and understanding to everyone who is involved with bulimia or anorexia through helplines, self-help groups, or individual membership (£20 pa) which includes an information pack and two monthly newsletters.

SCODA (Standing Conference On Drug Abuse), Waterbridge House, 32–36 Loman Street, London SE1 OEE, Telephone: 071-928 9500, is the national co-ordinating agency for services to illegal drug users. They refer drug abusers to suitable organisations in their area.

2
ADDICTIONS: WHAT THE GP CAN OFFER

Anyone can become addicted to a drug or particular type of behaviour, such as gambling or eating. The reasons why some of us do become addicted and others do not has been the subject of a great deal of medical research over the years, so much so that several scientific journals are devoted to the subject. Despite this, dependence on one substance or another, or compulsion to behave in a particular way, seems to be on the increase and there is still no satisfactory cure or set of actions which is guaranteed to help the person give up the habit.

The idea of addiction as a disease is one that has been used extensively in the last 20 years. It is one that many doctors are comfortable with, since it means that the person immediately becomes a patient, with all that implies about acceptance of advice and treatment. Equally, the person is then tempted to give up responsibility for their behaviour to some degree. Many non-medical agencies and support groups, such as Alcoholics Anonymous, continue to use this disease model as part of their group-therapy approach. In addition, it is acknowledged that there are often devastating social and economic consequences to alcohol addiction and other groups have been set up to help wives and children of alcoholics.

There is no doubt that the reasons behind addictive behaviour are complex and involve personal, social and economic factors, all of which need to be addressed if the individual is to make appropriate changes to their behaviour.

Many more family doctors now have some experience in psychiatry or training in dealing with psychological problems and they are more able to detect a problem in the early stages. Most of the common addictions, such as alcohol, smoking and even tranquilliser addiction, can be dealt with in General Practice by combining the skills of the GP, a specially trained nurse and, sometimes, a counsellor. Severe problems, however, in which the patient's physical health is endangered, will necessitate a referral to a specialist, usually a consultant psychiatrist or a consultant physician.

For some, the most help comes from outside agencies, either voluntary or those run by social services. The range and availability of these services varies from area to area but your doctor should be able to give you the information you need.

Not everyone wishes to confide in their GP about a behavioural problem, thinking they will be judged as weak or immoral. Not everyone will admit (or know) that they have a problem, especially with alcohol, even when faced with the medical evidence that the alcohol has done them physical damage. It all comes down to the kind of relationship you have with your family doctor. If they are sympathetic and you are able to trust them, it is far more likely that the relationship will be good and that the problem will be treated successfully. There is, however, quite a difference between GPs and the amount of help they will offer personally. If, after discussion, you are unhappy and do not seem to get on, try another GP in the same practice or register elsewhere. Remember, though, that the story will have to be told again from the beginning and also that, whoever is helping you, great effort is required on your part to come to terms with the problem and accept the need to change.

Alcohol

Asking about alcohol intake is now a routine part of screening within General Practice – for new patients registering, for those having a 'well-person' check and during a normal consultation with the doctor. Despite this routine questioning, several studies have shown that there is a large number of problem drinkers who do not come for help. When researchers looked at patients in three hospital wards, orthopaedic (concerned with disorders of the spine and joints), casualty and general medical, they found that at least 20% had an undiagnosed alcohol problem. Despite a hospital setting, or perhaps because of it, most of these patients did not get help at that time.

Heavy drinkers visit their GP more often than the average person, so the family doctor is in an ideal position to spot the problem and offer intervention. The practice nurse may also be able to intervene satisfactorily during screening or other routine nursing procedures. A medical professional who has an intimate knowledge of the family background is likely to be taken far more seriously than a complete stranger when asking questions and giving advice about drinking habits.

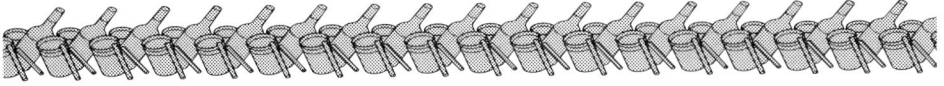

Many people who drink are genuinely unaware of the harm they may be doing to themselves and their families. It may not be the drinker who comes for help but a close relative, usually the wife, husband, son or daughter. It is then much more difficult to intervene, especially if the drinker is reluctant to attend the surgery. In such cases, relatives are usually advised to contact one of the voluntary agencies. The families of alcohol dependants have often spent many years tolerating difficult and violent behaviour and are ill-equipped to help and support the drinker in abstaining and coming to terms with life.

None the less, studies in General Practice have shown that the family doctor is very influential in bringing about change in drinking habits. It is a sad fact that many problem drinkers do not tell the truth about their drinking, so asking the right questions in the right way is important. The same applies to all those with destructive habits and addictions.

Fear of judgement is a major factor in stopping the drinker from getting help. So it is important that the doctor is non-judgemental in questioning and giving advice. This is particularly important when, as is commonly the case, the problem drinker has low self-esteem.

Asking for a day-by-day account of drinking can be very revealing, as well as the question, 'When did you last have a drink?' There are other key questions, too, that can sometimes trigger an admission to a serious habit, such as enquiring about memory loss after a bout of drinking, inability to stop drinking once started and whether the person has been made to feel guilty about the amount they drink.

Treatment

The type of treatment which a person with a drink problem will receive depends entirely on what they are prepared to accept. It is often the case that words of warning from family and friends are ignored but the doctor's advice is taken more seriously, especially when given in a clear and non-judgemental manner. Too often, though, people deny there is a problem, even when faced with evidence from a blood test or serious illness, and that physical harm is being done.

Studies of problem drinkers have shown that success in stopping is much more likely if the person has a supportive spouse, and a large part of the help the GP will give is in providing support and

guidance for family members. This includes, of course, referral to the appropriate agency, which may be a local support group or social services counselling agency. There are a number of ways in which the GP can intervene without prescribing drugs – it is only the minority of heavy drinkers who need and benefit from drugs. Non-drug interventions may include suggestions for reducing anxiety, either with relaxation classes which may be run from the surgery, or with alternative approaches described in later chapters in this book.

Drug Interactions

It is wise to be honest with your GP about how much you drink, as this can affect the dose and type of drug given. The functioning of the liver may be seriously impaired in heavy drinkers and this means that the action of some drugs is greatly prolonged. *Anticoagulants*, (blood-thinning tablets), for example, *warfarin*, can have an exaggerated effect and cause severe *haemorrhage* (blood loss). Inflammation of the stomach is a common occurrence in alcoholics and this could lead to bleeding and ulcers when combined with anti-inflammatory drugs, such as *ibuprofen* or *naproxen*. There are many other possible interactions as well.

Anxiety Management

Many problem drinkers may have failed to give up on previous occasions because they are using alcohol as a prop to stave off anxiety. Indeed, for some, this may be the root of the problem. So learning relaxation techniques can be very useful, especially during the early stages, and the skills will last a lifetime if they are practised regularly. Some surgeries will have a practice nurse or community psychiatric nurse attached who will give instruction either individually or in a group. If this is not available at your own doctor's practice, referral to the local hospital, perhaps to the psychiatric department, may be possible.

Drugs Used In Treating Alcohol Dependency

When any drug is prescribed, the GP needs to ensure it does not interact badly with alcohol. The ideal situation, of course, is that the person stops drinking alcohol altogether and is given the appropriate support and help so that no drugs, or only minimal

amounts, are necessary. As with any addiction, however, a great deal of anxiety may be created when the person thinks about withdrawal and some drugs are useful to relieve this anxiety in the early stages, as well as reducing the withdrawal symptoms themselves. All the drugs below should be given only as a course of treatment which starts and ends at a time agreed by the patient and doctor.

Disulfiram (Trade Name: Antabuse)

This drug is sometimes useful, especially for the treatment of alcohol-dependent people who have a tendency to drinking bouts. It comes in tablet form. Alcohol is broken down by *enzymes* (complex proteins) in the liver to the chemical *acetaldehyde*. Disulfiram prevents the further breakdown of this chemical so that it accumulates in the body when alcohol is taken. This causes flushing, headache, *palpitations* (rapid heart beats), nausea, faintness and even collapse if large quantities of alcohol are consumed. With this drug, the person needs to be under medical supervision, with regular visits to their GP or an out-patient department.

Chlormethiazole (Trade name: Heminevrin)

This is usually given in tablet form, though sometimes by injection, to damp down the effects of alcohol withdrawal. It has a sedative effect but also has the potential to become habit forming, so it is generally only used in short courses under close medical supervision.

Benzodiazepines (Trade Names: Diazepam, Nitrazepam, Etc.)

These have a very limited place in the treatment of heavy drinkers, for example, for someone who has a lot of anxiety about stopping drinking or who has acute withdrawal symptoms. These drugs will help to prevent shakiness and can aid sleep in the short term. They have an effect on the sleep pattern of the person, which takes time to return to normal after the course has finished. They should only be given for a very few days because of their addictive potential.

Beta-blockers (Trade Names: Propranolol, Atenolol, Tenormin, Etc.)

These drugs are used for a variety of illnesses including *angina* (sudden chest pain) and high blood pressure. Both of these conditions are more common in alcohol abusers and so the drugs may already have been prescribed. They slow the heart rate and reduce blood pressure. This means that they can prevent palpitations and sweating, to some extent, without causing drowsiness. They do not have the same addictive

potential as benzodiazepines. However, they should still only be given as a course, as the person may come to rely on them in the longer term, even though they are not physically addictive. They can have a variety of side-effects, including tiredness and nightmares. They can also make asthmatics more wheezy and should be given with great caution to this group of people.

Vitamins

Extra vitamins are essential for anyone who has had an alcohol problem for more than a few months. Many people who drink heavily tend to neglect their diet and are at special risk of deficiency of B vitamins. Vitamin B deficiency can manifest itself as damage to the brain with symptoms of confusion that can mimic dementia and other illnesses. When a person withdraws from a heavy alcohol intake, vitamins are usually given for a week or more by daily injection into the buttock muscle. Treatment is then continued with tablets for several months. In fact, recent studies have suggested that anyone who drinks heavily should have a vitamin supplement to prevent damage to the nervous system, whether or not they are withdrawing (see Chapter 3).

Referral To A Specialist

Alcohol can affect every system in the body, including the brain, but especially the liver, pancreas and bowel. Heart disease and diabetes are more common in alcohol abusers, as are *duodenal ulcers* (ulcers in part of the small intestine) and bleeding veins in the *oesophagus* (gullet), called *oesophageal varices*. There are many instances, therefore, where admission to hospital may be needed or the advice of a consultant specialist sought. This can be a turning point for some when the person finally realises that their life may be in danger.

Unfortunately, mental illness is also more common, especially depression, and the suicide rate in alcoholics is sadly high. Quite often the person will not realise that they are ill and it may be extremely difficult to persuade a friend or relative that they need help and medication. There is sometimes no alternative other than admission to a psychiatric unit and means exist to compulsorily admit a person as a last resort if they are a danger to themselves or others.

Tranquillisers

During the 1970s a group of drugs which relieved anxiety and helped sleep became available on prescription. Millions of prescriptions were issued for treatment of *agoraphobia* (fear of public or open places) and panic attacks but they were also given for prolonged periods following, say, the death of a loved one. They replaced other drugs, such as barbiturates, which were known to be highly addictive and dangerous in overdose. It was only years later that it became obvious to patients and their doctors that these seemingly harmless drugs were actually addictive.

Examples of these tranquillisers are Valium, Librium and Ativan, once household words, now better known by their generic names, such as *diazepam, lorazepam, temazepam* to name but some. Public awareness has increased greatly in the last 20 years and although now most people are very aware of the dangers of these tablets there are still many people, particularly in their middle years, who experience great difficulty in withdrawing from them. GPs now prescribe them far less and only under supervision. They have a part to play as an interim measure for someone who is extremely anxious or distressed, or who cannot sleep, until the root cause of the problem can be uncovered and addressed. They should not be confused with antidepressant tablets, for example, *amitryptilline* and *prothiaden*, which may be prescribed for depression or to help chronic pain. These work in a completely different way in the body and are thought to have virtually no addictive potential.

For severe agitation or mental illness another group of drugs exists, known as major tranquillisers. Examples of these are *chlorpromazine* and Melleril (trade name). They should always be taken as prescribed and will generally be given as a course, possibly under the supervision of a specialist. Your doctor should make it clear which type of drug you are being given and for what reason and for how long. If you have any worries about drugs you are prescribed, ask your GP for clarification.

The First Step

It is now routine practice for family doctors to supervise anyone on long-term medication, for whatever reason. It may be the person has been prescribed tranquillisers for years for a particular fear or phobia because other treatments have failed, and it is only when a

new doctor joins the practice that the prescription is questioned. It may be a threatening experience to be called in to see a new doctor but it is highly unlikely that any tablets would be suddenly stopped. You should be able to discuss with your doctor a method of reducing their intake, over which you have control. Approaching the doctor yourself is, of course, a far better way and more likely to succeed. Talking to the practice nurse at the surgery beforehand or making a list of questions and worries is helpful and will help your doctor to draw up a withdrawal plan with you.

Withdrawal Symptoms

These can be very varied. Some are unusual, such as aching in the jaw; more typical are shakiness, irritability, poor sleep and depression. There are many other symptoms which you may or may not experience. It sometimes helps to write them all down and discuss them with your doctor. Whatever the symptom, it is certain to pass with time and should be considered as part of the healing process.

Stopping Suddenly
This is the ideal situation if you can face it but is not always advisable. Anyone who is taking 5 mg of diazepam per day or equivalent can stop safely and expect very little in the way of symptoms. At higher doses than this, coming off should be a slow process, as described below.

Changing The Tranquilliser
It may seem a strange idea to consider swapping one drug for another but it seems to help. Most people are better off changing their benzodiazepine to diazepam. This is because it is a long-acting drug and therefore less likely to cause withdrawal symptoms as the dose reduces. Your doctor will usually decide the equivalent dose.

Other Drugs

Occasionally beta-blockers are used to help with the symptoms of anxiety and palpitations, for example, *proranolol* and *atenolol*. These are given as a course over a number of weeks. They slow the heart rate and lower blood pressure without causing drowsiness. Some people benefit from antidepressants if depressive symptoms are persistent or severe. A course usually lasts a minimum of 6 weeks

and is then tailed off slowly. They can be given at the same time as benzodiazepines.

The Withdrawal Plan

This should be made together with your doctor, taking into account your needs and worries but also bearing in mind the knowledge your GP has about the drug and about you personally. It should ideally be a compromise that still allows you to feel in control. The plan should state in detail how much and how often the dose is to reduce, so that there is a known endpoint when you should be drug free. Having a goal date really does help, as does giving yourself a reward when you get there, such as a holiday. As a rule, reduction should be at the rate of approximately $1/8$ of the total daily dose of drug every 2 to 4 weeks. It can be speeded up in some people to double this if they are strongly motivated, but should not otherwise be any faster.

An important part of the plan will include how you will get the necessary outside support and treatment for the problem or phobia that led you to go on to tranquillisers in the first place. There may be a tranquilliser support group near you, for example, either at the local hospital psychiatric department or run by a voluntary agency. Counselling or psychotherapy may be appropriate and some practices provide this on their premises.

Taking Stock Of Yourself

Having made the decision to come off tranquillisers it is inevitable that many aspects of your lifestyle will need to change. Your general health is especially important and it may be a good time to have a routine check-up with your doctor or practice nurse. Your drinking, eating and exercise habits will usually be discussed at this time and you may find an increasing curiosity about your health as the effect of the drugs reduces. It is a good time to start exercising again, once the doctor has confirmed you are fit enough.

Your relationships will begin to change as you come out of the gloomy world that tranquillisers induce and certain problems may come to light that had been left for many years. Again a counsellor in the practice or specially trained practice nurse may help here. There is often a good deal of work to be done in order to 'grow up and out of' the tranquilliser habit.

Smoking

When asked directly by a doctor, most smokers will say that they want to give up, but taking the first step to becoming a non-smoker is often very difficult. Excuses abound about being unable to cope, putting on weight, becoming bad tempered, that the habit has been going on for so long that there is no point in giving up for health reasons, and so on. Even so, studies have clearly shown that the GP is more likely than anybody else to influence a person to stop smoking and more resources than ever are now available at the surgery, too, to provide help and support. You should be asked about your smoking habits by your doctor or the practice nurse, whatever your reason for attending, and many surgeries have information leaflets available as a focus for discussion about treatment to help you stop.

Surprisingly often, health is not the most persuasive reason for stopping, unless a serious medical condition is diagnosed. This is amazing considering that the link between lung cancer and smoking was discovered more than 30 years ago and it is common knowledge now that smoking causes chronic *bronchitis* (inflammation of the bronchial tubes) and heart disease. The argument that giving up smoking will not improve health because it has been a lifetime habit does not apply, because there is good evidence that the risk of lung cancer diminishes considerably for ex-smokers, even if they have smoked for many years.

The motivation to give up smoking is often due instead to social factors: the unpleasant smell of smoke on clothes and on the breath or the high cost of smoking. The essential factor is that the person should decide for themselves that they want to become 'smoke-free'. It is widely known that nicotine, the active ingredient in tobacco, is very much a drug of addiction – any heavy smoker will tell you that. Withdrawal from it can cause a variety of symptoms, including anxiety, insomnia and irritability. Many people also complain that their cough gets worse. This is mainly because the excess mucus produced by the air passages is not so easily got rid of without the irritant effect of the smoke. Once the person stops smoking, the amount of mucus decreases and the cough will eventually disappear, provided of course that there is no chronic bronchitis or *emphysema* (a condition in which the air sacs of the lungs are grossly enlarged), which permanently cause a lot of *phlegm* (mucus).

A general feeling of ill-health may also follow giving up smoking, while the body repairs itself and clears itself of toxic substances.

Most of these symptoms will disappear over a few weeks but some may persist for up to a year. Support is, of course, paramount and some of the products mentioned below come with a complete package including 'no-smoking' posters to put up at home, a telephone help-line for counselling and booklets containing advice. The surgery you attend may run a special support group or may offer individual sessions with the practice nurse or your GP to check on progress. A few enlightened General Practices have the services of an acupuncturist or aromatherapist on the premises and some GPs themselves may be qualified in these therapies or in hypnotherapy. The practice leaflet will tell you what is available.

Once the decision is made to stop, a nicotine substitute may be useful and the different types of these are described below. Originally, these were only available on private prescription but they have now been made available over the counter. Certain precautions are necessary when using them if you already have an illness, such as heart disease, diabetes, and *hyperthyroidism* (overproduction of the thyroid hormone by the thyroid gland), or if you take certain medication. Although this is explained in detail in the leaflets given out with the nicotine preparation, it is wise to consult your doctor before starting the treatment. Most GPs will then monitor treatment and offer support. Taking nicotine in this way can have side-effects, which include dizziness, nausea, insomnia, palpitations and indigestion. Most people tolerate treatment very well, however, and are prepared to put up with minor unpleasant effects for the long-term benefits to their health.

Aids To Giving Up Smoking

Nicorette Gum
Available in 2 mg and 4 mg pieces, this was the first preparation on the market and it is still popular because it is placed in the mouth, like a cigarette. Nicotine from the gum takes a minute or two to have effect, rather longer than a puff of a cigarette, but each piece of gum lasts up to half an hour. The maximum recommended dose is fifteen 4 mg pieces in 24 hours. Some people get a sore mouth or ulcers with it but this is unusual. Usually after 2 or 3 months, the person will wean themselves off the gum. In rare cases there is some difficulty doing this and it may then be wise to change to the nicotine patches. Anyone experiencing difficulty might be offered counselling in the practice or with a psychiatrist.

Nicabate/Nicorette/Nicotinelle TTS Patches

These are similar patches but produced by different pharmaceutical companies. They are made with a pouch which contains the nicotine in solution. The side which goes next to the skin is made of a membrane which allows slow release of the drug. Nicotine is absorbed through the skin at a constant rate, which means that levels of nicotine in the blood remain fairly constant, avoiding withdrawal symptoms. Nicorette patches are used for 16 hours at a time and removed at night, while the other two preparations last 24 hours and are used continuously. Each preparation has three different strengths, for example, Nicotinelle TTS comes in 15 mg, 10 mg and 5 mg doses. The highest strength is used first and is replaced after 3 to 6 weeks with the next highest dose, and so on until withdrawal is complete. Treatment is for 3 months in total, with a review by the doctor recommended if withdrawal from them is not complete by then.

Remember, whatever you use to help you, most people take more than one attempt to give up. It is worth trying again, even if you have lapsed for a few days or even some weeks.

Illicit Drug Use

Glue Sniffing

A particular problem among adolescents and also pre-teenagers, glue sniffing, or sniffing of any solvent, is a great worry to parents. It has indeed proved fatal in a small number of cases and can cause liver damage, but most users do not have lasting effects from the habit and many simply grow out of it.

The few who abuse solvents habitually may develop temporary personality changes, such as irritability and mood swings, along with drowsiness and a tendency to a runny nose, and their clothes may smell strongly of solvent. The euphoric effect lasts up to 3 to 4 hours. The family and young person need support, as it is often poor family relationships which underlie glue sniffing or, indeed, any drug taking. It may be possible to reach agreement to stop and provide support without seeking further, specialised, help. Family therapy with a psychiatrist may sometimes be of benefit and there is usually a regional centre for this if the local hospital does not provide it.

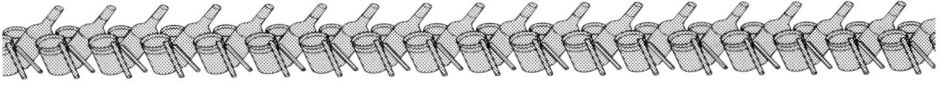

Marijuana

The use of this drug is increasing. Although it is not regarded as a drug of dependence, many doctors would say, that habitual use causes at least a psychological dependence if not the physical symptoms of other drugs. Psychological problems may take some time to resolve. The person has been away from reality so long that they have not had the chance to come to terms with their personal problems. The heavy use of marijuana over years is thought to increase the likelihood of mental illness. Again, the most important aspects of the GP's role are to provide support to the user and family, with appropriate referral to a counsellor or a consultant psychiatrist. There are no specific drugs which aid withdrawal. Driving under the influence of marijuana is particularly dangerous.

Heroin And Other Hard Drugs

The misuse of 'hard' drugs, such as heroin and cocaine, has been on the increase, especially over the last five years, and now most family doctors will come across at least one user during the course of a year, depending on where they practise. Like alcohol and smoking, it should be routine for the doctor to ask about drug use, though quite commonly addicts will come into the surgery and volunteer the information before asking for a prescription. GPs vary considerably as to how much they are prepared to help. It depends somewhat on the nature of the drug misuse, whether the patient is willing to agree a withdrawal regime and whether there are any associated medical problems. The picture is sometimes complicated by the tendency of drug misusers to be unreliable about completing courses of prescribed drugs and to relapse. Some GPs are then only willing to help if there is joint care with a specialist, usually a consultant psychiatrist with a special interest in drug problems.

The main task of the family doctor is to encourage the person to seek appropriate help, whether by admission to a specialised hospital or at home with the help of voluntary organisations or help groups run by social services. The GP is there to minimise the harm done by drugs with appropriate medical intervention, such as treating infections, and to support the person into their drug-free state, usually with the help of drug substitutes. Many addicts suffer from other illnesses and infection with hepatitis and with AIDS is an increasing problem. These should be tested for with the person's consent. Once again, it is essential to make the best use of the

facilities available in terms of outside support, such as psychotherapy and counselling.

There is an enormous variation between different health districts regarding services available to drug misusers. If information from your doctor is not forthcoming, there is a 'directory of services' produced by each district and most voluntary agencies are advertised locally, if only in the telephone book. It is likely, though, that your GP will have more detailed information and will know where best to direct you.

Anyone who abuses drugs such as heroin, or even codeine, has to be notified to the Home Office and the GP must do this on a special form. Special prescription pads are available to GPs so that a daily amount of a substitute drug can be dispensed by the chemist. Specially licensed doctors may prescribe heroin to abusers but these doctors are few and are mostly based in specialist centres. A GP may prescribe it only in cases of disease or injury.

Below is a description of the type of drugs likely to be prescribed during heroin withdrawal. Other drugs, such as the hallucinogens Ecstasy and LSD, may be stopped without withdrawal effects, although tranquillisers can sometimes be helpful.

Methadone

This is the standard drug used as a substitute for heroin. It is most commonly used in liquid form but comes in *suppositories* (in solid form for insertion into the rectum or vagina) as well. These are used less often as they can be melted down and injected.

A simple formula is used to calculate the dose needed to replace the heroin and methadone is usually issued on a daily prescription, as described above, and taken once daily. The dose is then reduced, on a weekly or fortnightly basis. Methadone is itself potentially addictive but not nearly as much as heroin. It will prevent most of the worst withdrawal symptoms, that is, stomach cramps and sweating. It has side-effects similar to morphine and heroin and in a non-abuser would cause drowsiness, euphoria, constipation and other effects. Most abusers do not get these at all as they are used to heroin.

Benzodiazepines

These are given in short courses for severe anxiety only. Caution is needed as they may be sold illegally or injected.

Diphenoxylate (Trade Name: Lomotil) And Loperamide (Trade Name: Imodium)

Both these are commonly prescribed in General Practice to stop diarrhoea and stomach cramps.

Promethazine (Trade Name: Phenergan)

Although this is an *antihistamine* (often used in the treatment of allergies), it has sedative properties as well. It is not addictive and can therefore be useful where anxiety and insomnia are prominent. Apart from sedation, side-effects are rare.

Thioridazine (Trade Name: Melleril)

There are several similar drugs to this which are known collectively as major tranquillisers which are used extensively for psychiatric illness (see page 31). They are more powerfully sedative than promethazine and their side-effects are more common. Involuntary movements may occur at high doses and close medical supervision is necessary.

Conclusion

Your GP, then, can offer quite a lot of support to you and your family as you withdraw from your addiction. It may not be direct support, but a recommendation to a specialist or to a support group. Drug therapy can help the symptoms of withdrawal but you will also need to work on your emotions and mental attitude.

3

NUTRITION: FUNDAMENTAL TO RECOVERY AND GOOD HEALTH

In the following chapters we shall look at complementary health-care systems and their role in dealing with various addictions. These complementary therapies are capable of assisting you break the habit, sustaining you through the withdrawal period and helping you to stay off your addiction. Nutrition is also fundamental to recovery and to continued good health. People who are trying to break free from an addiction need to pay more attention to their diet than most.

Our bodies have not evolved to exist naturally in today's environment and the fact that we do places us under stress. We breathe in polluted air loaded with toxins, such as cadmium, carbon monoxide and nitrates, which poison our bodies. The immune system, our body's defence mechanism, has a full-time job trying to eliminate these poisons so that we do not suffer any major illnesses as a result.

The water we drink is loaded with chemicals which, while they succeed in removing any bacterial danger, are none the less introducing more chemical toxins which our bodies have to neutralise – again a job for the immune system.

Stress is an everyday part of our lives. The traffic jam on the way to and from work raises blood pressure. The offices in which we work do not use natural daylight but artificial lighting which strains our eyesight. Many of us use a computer terminal which again strains our eyes and can, if posture is incorrect, lead to muscular damage to our hands and arms, and the medical establishment recognises *RSI* (repetitive strain injury) as a serious health problem.

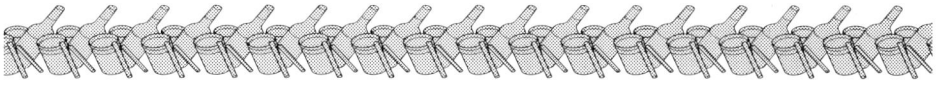

Some everyday triggers of stress

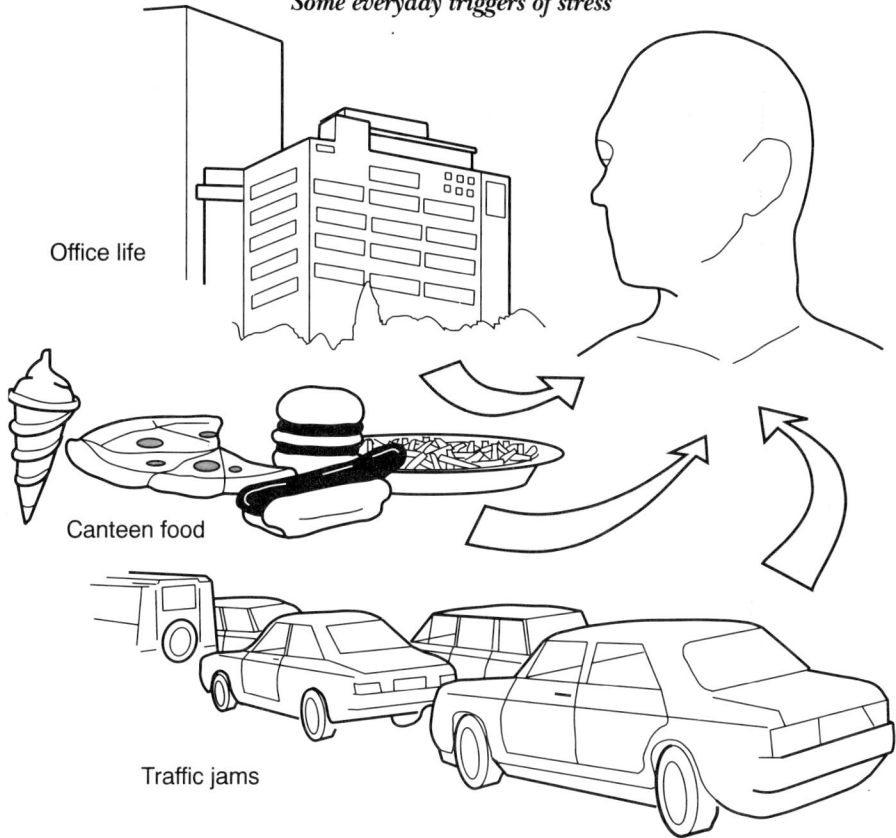

Office life

Canteen food

Traffic jams

The office canteen generally provides foods which are rich in refined carbohydrates and fats but short on vitamins and minerals. We rush home and, too tired or too late to go out and shop for fresh foods, pull something out of the freezer which comes out of its plastic wrapper and goes straight into the microwave. Or maybe we send out for a pizza or hamburger. You may ask 'what is wrong with a takeaway or convenience foods?' The answer is 'nothing', as long as they are eaten occasionally. If they form the mainstay of our diet then they become a problem: take a look at the ingredients' labels on convenience foods and sometimes you need a degree in chemistry to understand them. The truth is that convenience foods are made with highly refined foods which have been stripped of their original goodness and to which have been added chemical stabilisers, flavour enhancers and preservative chemicals to extend the shelf-life of the product. Eating such foods introduces yet more chemicals into the body for it to deal with.

In addition to the fact that a modern lifestyle places stresses on

our immune system, our bodies also have to contend with the shortfall of positive factors which it requires in order for our nervous system to function well. Stress is usually kept under control by metabolising the B vitamins which the nervous system needs in order to function. If, however, our diet is lacking in B vitamins, the nervous system is weakened. Further stress places more demands on the nervous system, which is already weakened, and it needs more B vitamins than it would normally. The situation is much like driving a car in winter with an old battery unable to cope with the daily power drain to start the car and power the lights and rear window heater. Unless you finally charge the battery it will simply conk out – leaving you high and dry! Of course, this is where the analogy ends, since you can simply go and buy another car battery to replace the exhausted one. You cannot go out and buy yourself a new nervous system.

A car needs a regular service, petrol, oil and correct handling to maximise its performance potential. Our bodies too need regular attention to the major parts of the system and daily attention to the correct fuel – a well-balanced diet – to function well.

Health and Nutrition: The Well-balanced Diet

By definition, a 'well-balanced diet' is one which provides us with the correct proportions of all the nutrients needed by the body to function efficiently and remain healthy.

A modern Western diet is high, often too high, in *macronutrients*: these are proteins, carbohydrates and fats – the 'bulk' foods, which provide energy, as well as other needs. However, our diets are typically short of the *micronutrients*: these are vitamins and minerals only needed in tiny amounts, yet equally vital to the body's functions. Since we know that fruit and vegetables contain essential vitamins and minerals, we logically conclude that consumption of these food products will maintain our required micronutrient levels, and before the age of technological farming and supermarkets, such a conclusion would have been valid.

Today's farming methods guarantee us a plentiful supply of cheap produce all year round. However, modern farming practice employs artificial fertilisers and pesticides, so the food which is harvested is not only grown in chemicals but also covered in them; the soil in

Guidelines For Healthy Eating

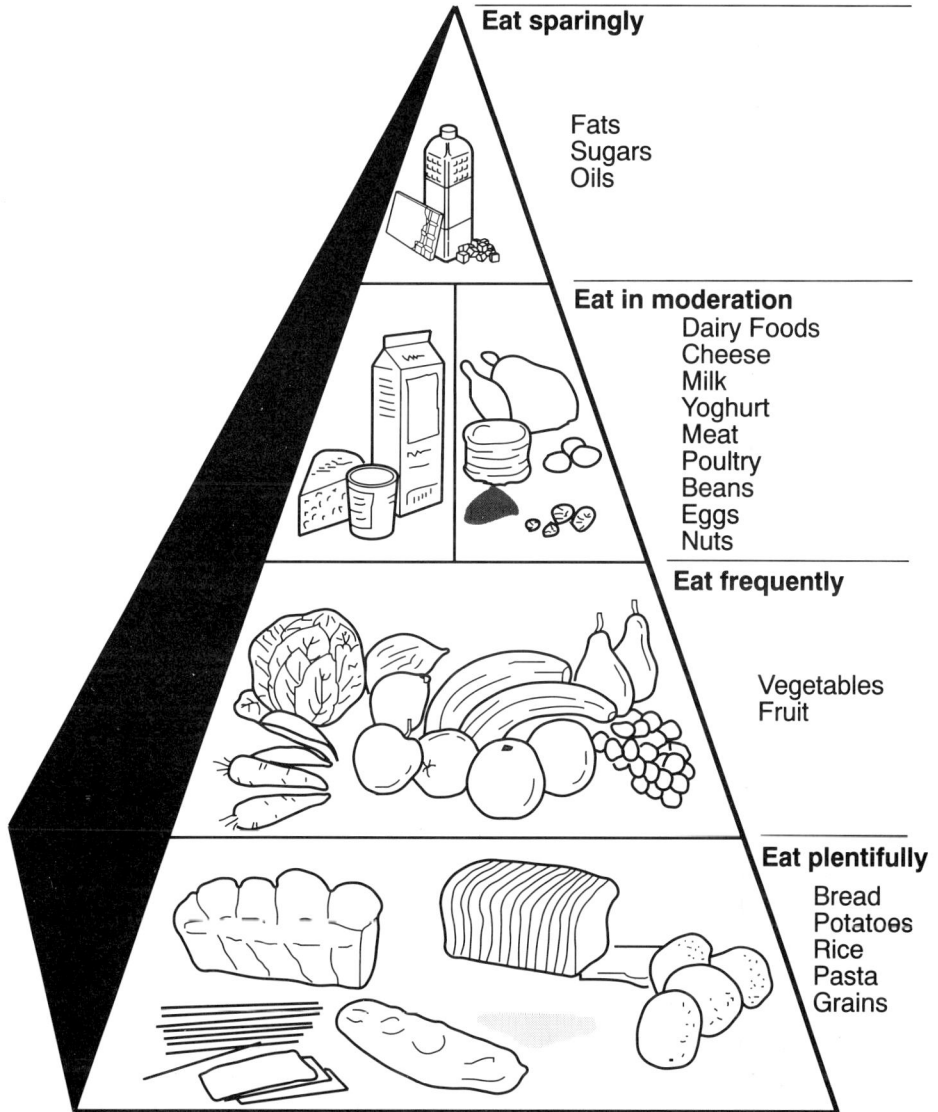

Eat sparingly

Fats
Sugars
Oils

Eat in moderation
Dairy Foods
Cheese
Milk
Yoghurt
Meat
Poultry
Beans
Eggs
Nuts

Eat frequently

Vegetables
Fruit

Eat plentifully

Bread
Potatoes
Rice
Pasta
Grains

The Healthy Eating Pyramid was evolved by nutritionists in the US. It has been adapted by the Dunn Nutritional Centre for application in Britain. It shows very clearly which foods we should be eating in large quantities and which we should be eating in only small amounts.

which our food is grown is exhausted (the old method of crop rotation is not economical when all the land can be used to produce food) and consequently the land is sometimes deficient in natural nutrients. After harvesting, produce is often treated with chemicals or perhaps radiation. Such treatments extend its natural life so that it survives transport and storage and has the shelf-life demanded by food retailers.

As consumers we buy this produce and then store it at home a little while longer, and when we come to cook it the methods which we use often leach out much of its vitamin or mineral content.

The end result is produce which looks and possibly tastes the same as it would have done if traditional production methods were used (although many would argue differently) but which may have reduced nutritional value. So, even though you may be eating your greens, they may not necessarily be providing you with much goodness!

To be sure of eating nourishing foods, you would need to grow them organically in your garden, or on your allotment, and pick them as you use them. Fifty years ago this was an everyday part of life, but not today. One alternative is to take vitamin and mineral supplements while following a nutritionally balanced diet with a large quantity and variety of vegetables and fruit.

Nutrition And The Immune System

How do vitamins and minerals contribute towards good health? If you consider that vitamin C is linked to warding off the common cold, the vitamin B complex to a healthy nervous system and garlic to lowering blood cholesterol, the connection between diet and true health begins to emerge. Particular vitamins and minerals are needed to maintain the immune system. When the body's immune system is no longer functioning it becomes susceptible to illnesses of every kind until it is finally debilitated to such an extent that recovery is no longer possible.

Research over the last decade is emerging to show that a particular group of micronutrients, called *antioxidants*, are effective in building up and maintaining the body's immune system. The antioxidants are vitamins A (especially the beta-carotene found in plants which the body can turn into vitamin A), C, E and the minerals selenium and zinc.

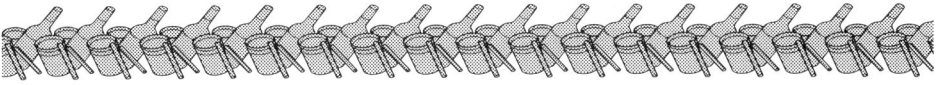

The Structure Of The Immune System

The immune system is the body's defence against both major and minor illnesses. When the immune system is functioning correctly, any germ which enters the body is destroyed by the body's army of fighter substances called *antibodies*. The antibodies even remember organisms so that future encounters are dealt with more rapidly if they occur again. This is called *acquired immunity* and vaccination uses this technique to safeguard us against certain diseases. As long as the immune system is healthy it can fend off the onslaught of disease. But it can be compromised by poor diet, environmental pollution, stress and even the natural process of ageing, with serious consequences. Sometimes, when the immune system malfunctions, it becomes overactive and starts attacking harmless foreign substances. Hay fever is a classic example. Normally pollen is harmless and yet the immune system starts to attack pollen particles. The cells involved in allergic response come out in full force, releasing histamine, resulting in the symptoms of hay fever.

At times the immune system goes horribly wrong and actually starts attacking the body's own cells. Rheumatoid arthritis is just such an example. Problems also arise in organ transplants because the immune system, programmed to reject foreign tissue, begins to attack the new heart or kidney.

You can see how important it is to keep the immune system in a state of balance. However, the problem for the immune system in this late twentieth century is that, while the human body is remarkably adaptable in its quest for survival, it needs time to change.

Unfortunately, the pace of change in the environment has overtaken the body's natural ability to offer a timely response. The immune system is overworked and does not always know how to respond to the array of new enemies that confront it. Environmental pollution, the depletion of the ozone layer, pesticides and CFCs have all contributed in upsetting our finely tuned immune system.

Furthermore, if the system cannot eliminate and detoxify a foreign organism the body has to store it somewhere. The liver, bones and even the brain, become the storehouses for this, sometimes dangerous, waste. The effects of these toxins, together with the imbalance of nutrients in our food, increases our vulnerability to disease.

How The Immune System Works

White blood cells form the defensive arsenal. They are divided into subgroups, each with a specific responsibility to defend us against the onslaught of disease. The *T-cells (T-lymphocytes)*, for example, have a regulatory function. The *B-cells (B-lymphocytes)* secrete highly effective antibodies. If there is a breakdown in any of the components of the immune system, the body's ability to fight disease is severely impaired. The result is that many of us live with recurring health problems – colds, flu, chronic fatigue and other diseases, including hay fever and asthma.

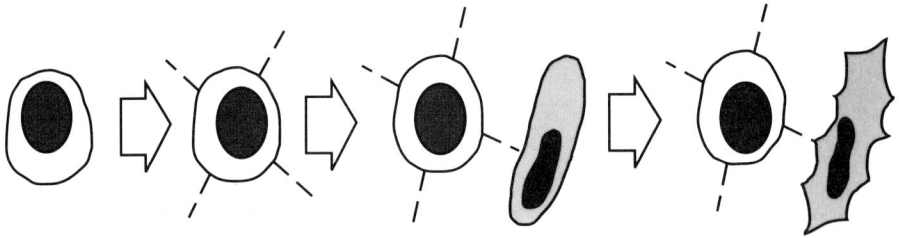

| 1. As soon as the immune system perceives an invading organism such as a virus, a killer cell called a *T-lymphocyte*, or a *T-cell*, is activated in the thymus. | 2. This activated T-cell is then released into the blood stream to find the invading organism. | 3. Once the T-cell locates the cell infected by the virus it locks itself onto it. | 4. Finally the T-cell breaks down the wall of the invader cell, thus destroying the invading organism. |

How the immune system works

What Compromises The Immune System?

One factor which can damage the immune system is the unchecked growth of *free radicals*. All living things which use oxygen produce free radicals continuously. Small amounts of free radicals are necessary for good health: they destroy disease-causing bacteria. But because they are electronically unbalanced molecules, they try to stabilise by combining with other molecules which carry an unpaired electron. This sets up a chain reaction because an otherwise stable cell becomes unstable when a free radical joins it; the destabilised cell goes on to attach itself to another cell in an attempt to stabilise again. This chain reaction can damage *DNA*, the all-important genetic building-blocks of life: the possible consequences of this are numerous and include cancer, memory loss, senility, ageing and *auto-immune diseases* (disorders suspected of

being caused by inflammation and destruction of tissues by the body's own antibodies).

Usually the production of free radicals is kept in check by the body's immune system but if the immune system is damaged it cannot destroy these potentially harmful molecules. Free radicals are released in their trillions in each puff of cigarette smoke, so smoking is very harmful indeed to health. Free radicals are also present in high quantities in polluted air and are formed by some pesticides and industrial solvents, and can be produced by excessive exposure to X-rays and radioactive contamination. There is increasing evidence that the antioxidants (see page 52) protect us from free radicals.

Special Dietary Requirements For Addicts

We have seen that nutrition is important for the immune system, even in a person who is not addicted to a damaging substance. Someone coping with substance dependency has an even higher requirement for correct nutrition.

Alcoholics, for example, are inclined to be malnourished because they do not eat properly or even regularly, often favouring alcohol over food. Alcohol affects every cell in the body. It also depresses the immune system. The liver breaks down alcohol to excrete it from the body, but since alcohol damages the liver, progressive drinking leads to accumulated alcohol in the body. The liver also produces bile which is responsible for the emulsification, digestion and absorption of fats and fat-soluble vitamins, as well as secreting enzymes to break down toxins. Consequently, the body cannot absorb the nutrients crucial to sustaining its functions, and neither can it successfully eliminate poisons. Damage to the liver is therefore fundamentally detrimental to health.

Excessive urinary loss, associated with drinking, exacerbates the difficulty of nutrient absorption. Zinc and magnesium are depleted by alcohol consumption; since these minerals are vital to every part of the body, from the reproductive system to the hair on your head, this has widespread consequences. Essential and immediate supplementation for people with a drinking problem would include high dosages of B-complex vitamins for their effects on the nervous, circulatory and digestive systems. Doctors may prescribe injections of B-complex vitamins with extra B_{12}: an injection enables the effects of some of the nutrients to be felt within hours. Further

supplementation would include magnesium, zinc, essential fatty acids (see page 48), protein supplements (for liver and brain function and regeneration of liver cells), vitamin C and lecithin.

Dietary recommendations for alcoholics

Increase:

fresh juices
carrot, beetroot and lettuce

Avoid:

fried foods, fatty foods, rich foods, chocolate, nuts, coffee, sugar, hot foods, chilli, spicy foods, dried fruits

Supplements:

beta carotene : 15 to 30 mg
vitamin B complex 100 mg
vitamin C 1 to 3 g
vitamin E 400 i.u.
magnesium 450 mg
selenium 200 mcg
zinc 20 mg, balance with copper 1 to 2 mg
evening primrose oil 2 to 3 g
L-glutamine, 2 g in divided doses when craving alcohol

Smokers, with each cigarette, introduce the following substances into their bodies: nicotine, carbon monoxide, carcinogens, hydrogen cyanide and trace gases. Trillions of free radicals are released with each inhalation of cigarette smoke.

Carbon monoxide combines with *haemoglobin* (red blood cells which transport oxygen from the lungs to the body's tissues, and transport carbon dioxide from the tissues back to the lungs for exhalation) and stops the haemoglobin from carrying out its function. Carbon monoxide also allows cholesterol deposits to collect on artery walls. These two factors account for the fact that smokers are at a high risk of heart attacks and strokes. Nicotine stimulates the heart, making it pump harder and faster (the 'rush' feeling), placing undue stress on it. Hydrogen cyanide inflames the bronchial linings which can result in bronchitis.

Supplementation to strengthen the smoker's weakened immune system must include vitamins A, C, E and zinc and selenium. Smoking actively depletes the body's supply of vitamin C. The

B-complex vitamins are essential to help repair the damaged nervous system, muscle tissue and heart. Research has shown that smokers tend to have poor diets. Unfortunately, this further compromises their health but supplementation and a healthy diet while trying to give up smoking will strengthen the body and make it easier to cope with withdrawal symptoms.

Tranquillisers deplete the body of the B vitamins when they are most needed, since B vitamins are constructive in reducing stress and irritability as well as playing other roles in health, vitamin C, several minerals and amino acids.

Excessive **caffeine** intake reduces the body's ability to absorb zinc and iron, so particular attention must be given to increasing these micronutrients. Too much coffee can cause a toxic accumulation of cadmium. (Naturally, the elimination of built up toxins is vital to all the addictions.)

The **hard drugs**, heroin and cocaine, not only reduce appetite but can produce a craving for sugar. Food which is eaten, therefore, tends to be calorie laden but not nutritionally laden, for example, cakes, biscuits, chocolate, ice-cream, crisps, fizzy drinks, refined foods, pizzas, and other convenience 'ready-to-eat' foods.

Specific deficiencies in vitamin C, B-complex vitamins and the minerals magnesium and zinc are common in hard drug addicts. Again, these deficiencies can be corrected with attention to diet.

People with a **sugar** or **food addiction** can ease their addiction by eating foods which are sustaining, rather than giving a short-lived buzz. A bar of chocolate will provide energy for 20–30 minutes; a muesli bar for a few hours. Chromium, manganese, vitamin C and zinc have been shown to reduce sugar-craving by stabilising blood-sugar levels.

Common Problems: How Diet Can Help

Hypoglycaemia

A predominantly nutritional disorder, *hypoglycaemia* literally means 'low blood glucose level'. Symptoms include fatigue, heart palpitations and an accelerated heartbeat, apprehension, dizziness, restlessness, hunger and nervousness.

During the process of digestion all the sugars and starches in our food are converted to glucose. If there is a high intake of sugars, the pancreas secretes insulin to enable glucose to be stored in the liver.

The pancreas also produces a hormone called *glucagon* which releases glucose back into the bloodstream, from the liver, to raise blood-sugar levels when necessary. This is to maintain the correct level of glucose in the body at all times. When this delicate system is upset, hypoglycaemia occurs. Among other factors, excessive consumption of alcohol, tobacco and caffeine can contribute to hypoglycaemia. So people suffering dependency on these substances are at special risk of developing hypoglycaemia. The best advice is to avoid all sugary foods, processed foods and junk foods and eat plenty of fruit, vegetables and grains.

Refined sugar causes the blood-sugar level to rise rapidly and this triggers the pancreas to over-secrete insulin, which will cause excess glucose to be stored as glycogen. While the sugar is quickly used up, the insulin continues to circulate in the blood for several hours. This has the effect of lowering the levels of sugar in the blood and triggers a craving for more sugar. If the hypoglycaemic eats more sugar it deepens this vicious circle.

Liver Dysfunction

The liver is the largest internal body organ and is the prime site for metabolism: that is the breaking down and building up of molecules. It is also responsible for bile production: bile absorbs fats and many of the vitamins and eliminates many toxic substances. Unfortunately, drugs, alcohol and toxic chemicals impair the liver's ability to function, which affects overall body health. In the case of alcohol, for example, the liver begins by turning the alcohol into a substance which can be absorbed by the body and used as a source of energy. Too much alcohol swamps the liver and in time it becomes enlarged by fatty deposits. This affects its ability to function, so that less and less alcohol can be processed – to the alcoholic this effectively means that it takes less alcohol to get drunk. If the problem continues, cirrhosis of the liver will result: this is irreversible scarring to the liver – its cells are killed and no longer able to regenerate – the end result being the liver's complete malfunction. Cirrhosis of the liver results in death unless a new organ can be transplanted. While dead liver cells cannot be regenerated, stopping drinking, in conjunction with a nutritional policy to detoxify the liver and the entire body, can ease the liver back into good health.

Malnutrition

This is common to all addicts because, they are so focused on their addiction, that food is forgotten, and when their attention does turn to food it is unlikely to be a wholefood, nutrient-rich choice. Since some addictions deplete the body of zinc; this in itself reduces appetite. Ex-smokers find that in the period immediately after tobacco withdrawal their appetite returns and with it the likelihood of weight gain. However, weight gain can be avoided:

• if the digestive system is working properly (B-vitamins are required for this);
• if the diet is rich in wholefood, fresh fruit and vegetables, and high-fat, high-calorie food choices and refined foods are avoided;
• if exercise is taken regularly.

Depression

Addiction or depression: which comes first? What is clear is that certain addictions deplete the body of the B-complex vitamins, B_6 and magnesium, lack of which induces PMS (*premenstrual syndrome*) in women, irritability, stress and tension. So an addict may take a substance to relieve depression, ironically, only to worsen it. Further, the very nature of addictions is to create a cocoon into which the addict all too easily retreats, compounding the very factors which created the need for escape in the first place.

A Weakened Immune System

The white blood cells, the body's protective 'army', rely on vitamins A, B_6 and C to function well, and we have already seen how malnutrition is a common factor in addicts. Further, the over-production of free radicals as a by-product of substance addictions also weakens the immune system. The thymus gland is weakened by stress and the thymus is the main factor in the immune system. It is responsible, among other things, for production of several hormones which regulate many immune functions. Since people often turn to addictive substances to help them cope with the stress in their lives, the immune system suffers as a result. Anti-stress nutrients can combat the effects of stress.

Treatment

For all addiction withdrawal there are common steps to take to ease the process:

- Improved diet during active addiction: to build up the body's defence system and reduce the shock to the body when withdrawal begins.
- Continued attention to diet during withdrawal: it is important to keep helping your body expel the toxins and readjust to normal functioning.
- Nutrition to keep off the addiction: diet will reduce your craving for the addictive substance and eventually even your desire for it.
- Exercise to improve the body's metabolism: toning up the circulatory system, improving muscle tissue, increasing the brain's production of endorphins and hence promoting self-image and self-confidence.
- Counselling or psychotherapy to deal with emotional problems which led to the addiction; building self-confidence and self-esteem.
- Alternative therapies to promote the body's natural healing systems and reduce tension and stress.

Nutrients To Restore Health And Vitality

Antioxidants

Vitamin A And Beta Carotene (Pro-Vitamin A)
- Responsible for growth and maintaining an active thymus.
- Food sources: liver, carrots, green leafy vegetables, milk and butter.

Vitamin C
- An antiviral, it boosts production of *prostaglandin E1* (a compound which stimulates the muscles and affects the nervous system) and increases T-lymphocytes. It detoxifies many bacterial toxins and increases production of *interferon* (proteins made by cells in response to virus infection that prevent the growth of the virus).
- Food sources: potatoes, fruit juice, citrus fruit and green vegetables. The vitamin C content of these foods is affected by over-cooking (vitamin C leaches into water), the season, variety and freshness of the food. As a general guideline, foods which are at their freshest and eaten raw or lightly steamed with, in the case of root vegetables, the skin left on, will retain more of their vitamin C content.

Vitamin E

- Neutralises free radicals and hence protects against the effects of air pollution. Vitamin E combines with other nutrients to improve resistance to infections.
- Food sources: wheatgerm, green leafy vegetables, sunflower seeds, almonds and safflower oil.

Other Nutrients

Iron

- Without iron antibodies, the immune system's defence cells cannot be produced. Iron is essential in the activation of the enzyme used by white cells to attack foreign bodies.
- Food sources: lamb's liver, dried apricots, wholemeal bread, corned beef and egg yolks.

Selenium

- Selenium protects against the effects of free radicals and from the toxic effects of mercury, arsenic, cadmium and lead. It is required in the production of antibodies and by the white cells to recognise invading organisms, so a lack of selenium will affect the immune system. An anti-carcinogen, selenium is also used to keep the heart healthy.
- Food sources: offal, fish and shellfish, wholegrains and cereals and dairy products.

Zinc

- This mineral is found in the muscles, liver, kidneys and eyes, and in men in the prostate gland and sperm. Zinc functions in more enzymatic reactions than any other trace mineral: zinc deficiency therefore has numerous effects throughout the body.
- Food sources: oysters, brewers' yeast, shellfish, wholemeal bread, beans and pulses, and rice.

Magnesium

- Magnesium helps in reducing stress. 65% of the body's magnesium is found in the skeleton. It is necessary for calcium, phosphorus, sodium, potassium and vitamin C metabolism, the conversion of

blood sugar to energy, DNA replication, nerve and muscle functioning.
- Food sources: figs, lemons, grapefruit, almonds, seeds and wholemeal bread.

The B Vitamins

The B-complex Vitamins

- These are B_1, B_2, B_3, B_5, B_6, biotin, folic acid and B_{12}. All are water soluble and therefore cannot be stored by the body: daily intake of these vitamins is required to maintain satisfactory levels.

B1 (Thiamine)

- There is an increased need for this during stress or illness – it is a morale-boosting vitamin because it acts on the nervous system. It improves digestion, mental attitude and aids the functioning of the nervous system, muscles and heart.
- Food sources: yeast extract, soya beans, pork chop, rice, wholemeal bread, potatoes and milk.

B₂ (Riboflavin)

- There is an increased need for this during stress. It promotes healthy skin, nails, hair, good vision, growth and reproduction.
- Food sources: milk, liver, kidney, eggs, leafy green vegetables and fish.

B₃ (Niacin)

- This fights against tiredness, lethargy, depression and loss of memory, and can lower blood fat levels.
- Food sources: meat and meat products, potatoes and wholemeal bread.

B₅ (Pantothenic Acid)

- B_5 is involved in energy release from foods and is vital for the healthy functioning of the adrenal gland and in antibody formation.
- Food sources: brewers' yeast, yeast extract and nuts.

B₆ (Pyridoxine)

- B_6 is used in the assimilation of protein and fat, and prevents skin and nervous disorders. It reduces cramps and is a natural *diuretic* (an agent that increases the flow of urine).
- Food sources: brewers' yeast, bran, wheatgerm, liver, kidney, green leafy vegetables, dairy products and beef.

B₁₂ (Cobalamin)

- This is used in the production of red blood cells (it is therefore effective against a type of anaemia), promotes growth and appetite, increases energy and maintains a healthy nervous system, relieves irritability, improves concentration and memory, and is required for the assimilation of fats, carbohydrates and protein.
- Food sources: liver, beef and brewers' yeast.

Fats

Types Of Fats

- There are two types of body fats: *storage fats* and *structural fats. Storage fats* are predominantly saturated fats derived from dietary fats and carbohydrates. They ensure a long-term supply of energy in times of food or energy shortage and can be metabolised to energy by the body when food is short. *Structural fats* are mainly polyunsaturated fats.

Polyunsaturated Fats

- These are found in plants, vegetables and some fish, and are used in metabolic processes. These fats cannot be produced by the body.
- Polyunsaturated fats are converted to *GLA (gamma linolenic acid)* and *EPA (eicosapentaenoic acids)* although this process is hampered by age, diet and hormonal condition. A direct supply of GLA , however, is obtainable from evening primrose oil and borage, while a direct supply of EPA is available from fish oils. Both GLA and EPA are available in capsule form from healthfood shops. Evening primrose oil has been available on the NHS for treatment of eczema since the late 1980s.

- One of the main functions of polyunsaturated fats is as precursors to prostaglandins. Prostaglandins are hormone-like substances; their role in the human body is in regulating blood pressure and stimulating the immune system, promoting and reducing inflammation.
- Food sources: mackerel, herrings, sardines, tuna, salmon, evening primrose oil and borage.

Garlic

- Garlic possesses antiviral and antibacterial properties. It can also enhance the activity of the lymphocytes. In 1988 a Florida pathologist, T. Abdullah, demonstrated in an experiment the effect of garlic on natural killer cells. Dr Abdullah randomly divided volunteers into three groups. Over a three-week period one group took raw garlic, one group took aged garlic extract and the third group took no garlic at all. At the end of the three weeks, Dr Abdullah took blood samples from each volunteer and tested the natural killer cells in the blood against tumour cells in test tubes. The natural killer cells of those who took raw garlic killed 139% more tumour cells than those who took no garlic. And the natural killer cells of those who took aged garlic extract killed 159% more tumour cells than those in the control group.

Glutamine

- This is one of the 22 naturally occuring amino acids. Together with glucose, it is a major nourisher of the nervous system. It is popularly known as 'brain fuel'.
- It has been shown to control alcoholism by reducing the desire for alcohol. It alleviates fatigue, depression, impotence, schizophrenia and senility. L-glutamine (the natural form of glutamine) is available as a dietary supplement from health food shops and chemists.

Nutrition For Alcoholism

The objective here is to eliminate toxins, stop damage to the liver, build up the liver's functioning ability, increase appetite and improve nutrient absorption and digestive ability.

Recommended Nutrients

- vitamin A and zinc: lack of zinc affects vitamin A absorption so their effects are interrelated and they should be taken together, and a deficiency in either can result in cirrhosis of the liver and impaired immune function;
- antioxidants: vital for the liver and to boost the immune system;
- B-vitamins;
- magnesium;
- essential fatty acids;
- glutamine.

Nutrition For Caffeine Addiction

Objectives are to reduce nervousness, irritability, lack of energy, appetite loss and insomnia.

Recommended Nutrients

- B-complex vitamins for nervousness, irritability and improved energy levels;
- tryptophan, from natural food sources only, such as milk, for insomnia;
- zinc for improved appetite and energy;
- vitamin C for improved energy.

Nutrition For Addiction To Smoking

Objectives are to reduce stress and irritability, and to stop damage to the immune system.

Recommended Nutrients

- vitamin C for stress reduction, increased resistance to infections and boosted immune system;
- antioxidants to boost the immune system;
- B-complex to reduce irritability, reduce stress;

Nutrition For Tranquilliser Addictions

Objectives are to reduce stress and irritability, reduce hypoglycaemia and restore depleted vitamin C levels.

Recommended Nutrients

- vitamin C to reduce stress and increase resistance to infection;
- B vitamins to reduce irritability and stress;
- magnesium to reduce stress;
- tryptophan, from such food sources as milk, to relieve insomnia.

Nutrition for Sugar and Food Addictions

Objectives are to sustain blood sugar levels and stabilise moods.

Recommended Nutrients

- B-complex and magnesium to reduce irritability and tension;
- chromium to stabilise blood sugar levels.

Nutrition For Hard Drug Withdrawal

Objectives are to boost the immune system, build up muscles, improve concentration, lessen fatigue and reduce stress and depression.

Recommended Nutrients

- vitamins A, C and E to boost the immune system;
- zinc, selenium, magnesium, chromium and glutamine to boost the immune system;
- B-vitamins to improve eyesight and concentration, lessen fatigue and depression, reduce stress and tension.

Finding A Nutrition Therapist

Dietitians can be consulted free via your GP, as there is one in every district, usually based at the main hospital. Many are keen to help people improve their eating habits. Or, for a list of practitioners or further information write, enclosing a SAE to:

The British Naturopathic and Osteopathic Association, 6 Netherall Gardens, London NW3 5RR;

The British Society for Nutritional Medicine, 4 Museum Street, York, YO1 2ES;

The Nutrition Association, 36 Wycombe Road, Marlow, Buckinghamshire SL7 3HX.

Further Reading

E for Additives by Maurice Hanssen (Thorsons)
How to Fortify Your Immune System by Donald Dickenson PhD
    (Arlington Books)
Naturopathic Medicine by Roger Newman Turner (Thorsons)
Vitamin Guide by Hasnain Walji (Element Books)
Vitamins, Minerals and Dietary Supplements: A Definitive Guide
    by Hasnain Walji (Headway)

4
HERBAL MEDICINE: PLANT POWER

We saw in Chapter 1 how proper management of your withdrawal will play a large part in easing you off your addictive substance. Usually complete cessation of the addictive substance places too much of a strain on the system, although your doctor or practitioner will advise you in your particular case. Generally, a gradual withdrawal is best advised since that places the least strain and stress both on your mind and your body; addiction depletes the body's overall health and attention to this is also necessary.

Herbal medicines are gentle, gradual and free from side-effects, but do not think that herbs are ineffective just because they are gentle: in fact, because they are natural and have a gentle action, they are far more beneficial to human health than chemical drugs.

Herbal medicine is particularly useful both during the withdrawal period and in sustaining good health during and after recovery. This is because herbs contain an important active ingredient in addition to other ingredients which balance the effect of the active ingredient. For example, dandelion root is a herbal diuretic which also contains high levels of potassium – potassium is lost from the body when diuretics are taken. Modern chemical diuretics, do not restore the body's lost stores of potassium: this has repercussions in the absorption of other minerals which are used by the body in its functions.

Herbal medicine is regaining credibility and popularity in the Western world. Until fairly recently, herbal remedies were viewed by many orthodox medical practitioners as 'hocus pocus' treatments, which is ironic, considering that many of today's chemical drugs are based on natural remedies (black willow is the basis of aspirin and steroids are synthesised from the active ingredient in the Mexican wild yam, for example).

Herbal medicine has, of course, been used for thousands of years, and is still practised widely in China and India today. The Egyptian pyramid builders took garlic to increase their strength and resistance to infection; Assyrian physicians have left us records which tell us that they prescribed liquorice for chest difficulties. During

the Middle Ages, monks were skilled in the use of herbal tonics and administered preparations to the sick, and by the seventeenth century herbal medicine was well documented – Culpeper's famous *Herbal* is still in print and read today.

Herbal Medicine Today

Throughout the ages herbal remedies have been respected and trusted – until the advent of synthetic drugs in this century, when modern medicine turned its back on the natural and allied itself with the artificial. As increasing evidence of the dangerous side-effects of chemical drugs came to light, both medical practitioners and laymen came to appreciate the natural, gentle healing qualities of herbal remedies which are less likely to produce dangerous side-effects.

The reason why herbs are safer than chemical drugs can perhaps be explained by the fact that chemical drugs are simply the active constituent of the herb in concentrated form. Herbs are used whole, so that the known active ingredient and the other protecting ingredients remain together.

Herbalism: Gentle And Effective

Synthetic drugs are often much quicker acting than herbal remedies. But is this good or bad? The body falls ill after a gradual build-up of toxins or depletion of essential healthy nutrients. Addictions do not take hold overnight, after all. So the body needs time to heal. Herbal remedies build up the body gently and over time. Synthetic drugs are designed to produce results within hours, which is not always the safest way of treating an illness or an addiction.

The Holistic Approach

Herbal medicine aims not only to cure the body of an illness but also to strengthen it against further illness. It tones up organs and nourishes the tissues and blood and helps the body to eliminate toxins and keep it in general good condition.

This is why a medical herbalist, if presented with a problem of, for example, constipation, will prescribe a remedy to ease the

constipation but will also consider why the constipation has arisen at
all. A remedy would be prescribed for the overall digestive system
and attention would be given to dietary changes. This method of
taking an overview of the person and their medical complaint has
led to the term 'holistic' medicine. Herbal medicine is just one
holistic method. A herbalist treats each person individually, taking
into account social and economic factors, and the skill lies in
understanding that what may work for one person may not
necessarily work for another.

What Is A Herb?

This is not such a silly question as you may think. We immediately
think of herbs as ingredients used in cooking, which of course is
quite correct. In the kitchen, herbs are usually limited to the leaves
or roots of a plant, and a cook would draw the line at including
fungi in a list of herbs! A medical herbalist derives healing power
from the same herbs as a cook, but also from any plant, or part of a
plant, which has medicinal qualities. Marigold flowers are used in
many skin complaints, lungwort moss as an *expectorant* (for the
removal of sputum from the lungs) which children can safely take,
the kernel of the kola nut is used to counteract depression and as a
stimulant. Flowers, tree bark, ferns, seaweed, lichen, fungi, seeds,
leaves, twigs and roots are all used in herbal medicine.

Pill Or Liquid?

Herbal preparations are made up in a variety of forms. They can be
infusions (herbal teas), pills, *tinctures* (medicinal extracts in a
solution of alcohol), *poultices* (applications for the skin), drops,
syrups or *vapours* (for inhaling) or even preparations for the bath.
The same herb prepared in a different way will have a different
potency and sometimes a slightly different effect. Again, the skill of
the practitioner is invaluable in prescribing exactly what is best for
you.

Herbal Remedies And Addictions

If you decide to visit a herbalist, what kind of remedies would they
be likely to prescribe?

In the case of **alcohol** addiction, there are many fortifying and

healing herbs for the liver, which of course is the main organ that is damaged. Dandelion root, milk thistle, artichoke, balmony, centaury, black root and bittersweet are the primary herbs which help to detoxify the liver and promote cell regeneration. At the same time, some of these herbs act as diuretics, so speeding the elimination of toxins. They are also beneficial in improving the appetite and calming the digestive system. For **caffeine addiction**, *carminatives* (for relieving flatulence) can ease over-active bowel movements and excess stomach acid. Carminative herbs are familiar to us as culinary herbs; ginger, wild yam and sweet flag might be prescribed. Since, in excess, caffeine intake produces hyperactivity and nervousness, the nervous system will benefit from some of the *nervine* herbs. These act in different ways, as stimulants or relaxants. Oats are one of the best ways of calming the nervous system and can be taken in their food form. Oats provide sustained energy, making it a little bit easier to do without that extra cup of coffee or mid-morning snack.

Coffee substitutes are increasingly available now, and Barleycup and Bamboo are very popular and suitable in this respect. Herbal teas, camomile to calm, rosemary to perk you up, are an excellent alternative to caffeine, as well as providing their natural remedial benefits.

If **smoking** is your problem, as well as prescribing herbs to strengthen the nervous system and reduce irritability, a medical herbalist may well suggest adding lobelia extract to your cigarette: the resulting alkaloid compounds produce a foul taste to discourage you from smoking.

Coming off **tranquillisers** can be eased by herbal remedies to support the nervous system, so that eventually tranquillisers can be withdrawn without any side-effects.

Different Classifications Of Herbs

Carminative Herbs – For The Digestion

Carminative herbal remedies are rich in oils which act on the wall of the gut. They ease flatulence and gastric pains by stimulating a sluggish digestive system back into action.

Some specific carminative herbs: fennel seeds, ginger root and caraway seeds.

Other herbs with carminative action: there are many, many herbs which stimulate the digestive system as well as performing other functions. Peppermint, aniseed, wild yam, golden seal, dandelion, meadowsweet, artichoke and balmony are some of the more common remedies.

Nervine Herbs – For The Nervous System

The nervous system can be overactive or underactive, and there are herbal remedies for both conditions. The nervine relaxants calm the system, the nervine stimulants stimulate it, and the nervine tonics generally tone up the nervous system and keep it in good working order. People who are coming off an addiction must avoid the nervine stimulants, which exacerbate feelings of edginess and irritability. On the other hand, addicts will find the calming effects of the nervine relaxants most beneficial.

Nervine Relaxants

These are the closest natural alternative to tranquillisers, so care should be taken not to dose yourself to a permanently tranquillised state!
Some nervine relaxant herbs include black cohosh, black haw, camomile, lavender, passion flower, rosemary and skullcap.
In addition, there are herbs which act on other parts of the body to promote relaxation, for example the muscles, and as we all know from a long hot bath, a relaxed body encourages a relaxed mind. A nervine herb which works both on the nervous system and the muscle tissue is valerian.

Nervine Tonics

These natural herbs can be used after recovery from an addiction to maintain the well-being of your nervous system, safeguarding against gradual ill-health and degeneration of the nervous system. Their gentle effects means that they can safely be taken on a long-term basis.
Oats are a primary nervine tonic which are also, of course, highly nutritious. Eat up your porridge every day and your body will notice the beneficial effects not only in the nervous system, but also in the circulatory system. Oats take a long time to be digested by the body which is why they make an excellent breakfast; the body takes 4 to 5 hours to digest oats which means that you benefit from a slow, continuous release of energy. Add fruit and nuts for extra energy and vitamins.
St John's wort is a nervine tonic which is taken as an infusion or tincture. It is also used externally for rapid healing and easing muscle tissue pain, such as sciatica and fibrositis.

Nervine Stimulants

The nervine stimulants should be used with care by anyone, but particularly by people trying to kick a dependency who are in a very fragile state and who need to be calmed rather than stimulated. It is better to use nervine tonics for their general health-giving properties on the nervous system than to hype yourself up with a nervine stimulant.

Nervine herbs include the kola nut, the coffee bean, the tea leaf and maté. All these herbs contain caffeine and so should be avoided.

Diuretic Herbs – To Increase Urine Production

Diuretics encourage the production of urine. The idea of this is to expel accumulated toxins: the heavy drinker experiences this effect as the more he or she drinks the more he or she needs to urinate in order to expel the toxins in alcohol.

Dandelion leaf, artichoke, bittersweet, apple, broom, corn silk, grapes, juniper, onions and parsley are all diuretics which can be eaten or prepared as teas or infusions.

Hepatic Herbs

The hepatic herbs work on the liver and there are many different herbs which are combined for various liver ailments. In common, though, hepatics stimulate the production of bile. A sluggish liver produces less bile and this obviously affects the entire body's functions.

Some hepatic herbs:

- Centaury is an appetite stimulant which may be necessary when the liver is damaged.
- Black root combines well with dandelion to ease liver problems and jaundice.
- Bittersweet is a powerful herb which should not be used without a practitioner's direction. It is effective in a variety of ailments including reducing liver inflammation and as a diuretic.
- Milk thistle regenerates the liver's cells.
- Artichoke is a gentle hepatic tonic which promotes the digestive system, stimulates liver cell regeneration and is also a diuretic.
- Centaury restores lost appetite caused by liver damage.
- Balmony stimulates the digestive system.
- Dandelion root, with its high natural potassium content, is a gentle hepatic and diuretic.

Chinese Herbal Medicine

Traditional Chinese herbalists tend to be confined to Chinese centres, practising mainly in the Chinese community. The 'modern' Chinese herbalists often combine herbal medicine with acupuncture.

Chinese herbal medicine is based on *yin* and *yang*. *Yin* qualities are associated with cold, passivity, inactivity and darkness. *Yang* qualities are associated with the opposite of *yin*, that is, heat, vigour, excitement, movement, activity and light. The principles of *yin* and *yang* are that one cannot exist without the other and that harmony is only possible when both are present. Chinese texts explain it thus: if *yin* and *yang* are not in harmony, it is as though there were no autumn opposite the spring, no winter opposite the summer. *Yin* and *yang* control each other and change or transform into each other. The relationships between people, herbs and their environment are also described in a *yin-yang* framework: a human being is a miniature of the entire cosmos and therefore is subject to the same cosmic laws. According to Chinese medicine, illness arises as a result of an imbalance between the *yin* and the *yang*. As such, treatment is based on correcting any imbalances and restoring the natural harmony of *yin* and *yang*. Maintaining good health is a matter of maintaining the balance of yin and yang and their qualities. For example, if *yin* dominates, the result is exhaustion, passivity and weakness; if *yang* predominates, the result is irritability, excitability and hyperactivity.

The yin-yang symbol

Traditional Chinese Medicine And The Human Body

The dual forces of *yin* and *yang* are present in the workings of the human body, for example the heart contracts (*yin*) and dilates (*yang*) each second that it functions; the lungs function to the balanced rhythm of inhalation and exhalation and we alternate between sleep and wakefulness. Chinese medicine views food as medicine and medicine as food. Perhaps this is why Chinese cooking uses many of the herbs and roots which are used to heal illness. This is all part of the Chinese principle of maintaining good health: in the West we say 'Prevention is better than cure' but whereas we do not seem to live by that maxim, the Chinese do.

Some Chinese Medicines

All-round Tonic: Ginseng

The root of the ginseng plant has been used in the East for thousands of years. It was so highly prized that at one time it was more expensive than gold.

It is used as a general tonic to maintain good health and as such is taken on a regular daily basis by millions of Chinese, and increasingly, Westerners. It is said to increase energy levels – Barbara Cartland attributes her record-breaking writing output to ginseng – and improve longevity, hearing, vision, stamina and virility.

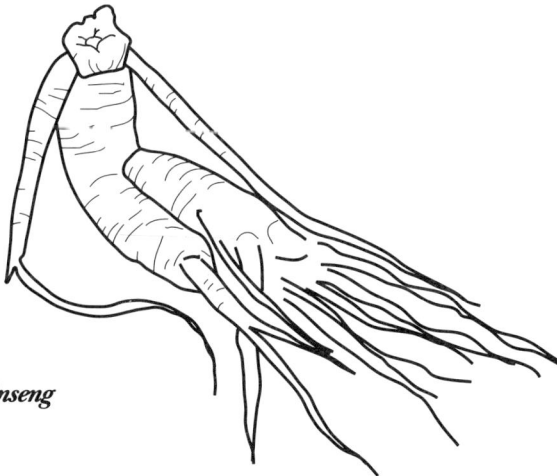

Ginseng

Scientific research has found that ginseng relieves hardening of the arteries (*atherosclerosis*), stabilises blood pressure, protects against radiation, stimulates and improves the brain cells' functioning, increases stamina and endurance, is anti-rheumatic and acts as an antidote to various drugs and toxic chemicals. In addition, it is beneficial in liver problems. All in all, it is a very wide-acting and powerful medicinal herb!

Ginseng root is available in various forms: capsules which contain the powdered extract, powder, the original root, fluid extracts, concentrated fluid extracts and even tea-bags. Because of its stimulating effect, it should not be taken just before going to bed as it is likely to keep you awake. Acidic fruits (oranges, grapefruit, lemons, grapes and strawberries), their fruit juices and vitamin C supplements, should be avoided for three hours after taking ginseng as they neutralise ginseng's effects.

There is little doubt that ginseng does have beneficial effects on the body, and for people who are trying to give up an addiction its effects on stamina, the liver and overall health make it most worthwhile to take. However, it is best not to take it for more than 6 to 8 weeks without advice from a qualified herbal practitioner.

For Stress And Insomnia: Catnip

Catnip is one of the mint family of herbs. Prepared in a tea, catnip is combined with oats, valerian and celery seeds to soothe stress, relieve a nervous headache and promote sleep.

For Edgy Nerves, Insomnia And Stomach Problems: Hops

The common wild hop contains an active ingredient called *lupulin*. Lupulin has a soporific effect and for this reason both Western and Chinese traditions use hops in pillows to encourage sleep. However, it might be more convenient to simply take a cup of hop tea: an ounce of hops is simmered for 2 to 3 minutes, left to stand for 5 minutes and strained. The tea is also effective in relieving indigestion and encouraging a poor appetite; since there are no unpleasant side-effects, hop tea is very beneficial for alcoholics, people coming off tranquillisers and caffeine addicts especially, who can enjoy hop tea as an alternative to coffee or tea. Since hop tea is very bitter, you should sweeten it with honey but not sugar, since sugar will only artificially raise your blood sugar levels and leave you fatigued later. **Do not take hops if you are depressed.**

For Relief Of Nervousness, Stress, Etc: Eleutherococcus Senticosus (Eleuthero)

A tall shrub which grows in the wild in the Far East, eleuthero is used as a tonic and as a remedy for nervousness, stress, exhaustion, moodiness and depression. It is therefore useful for all addicts as they come off their particular addiction. Available from health food stores, you can take eleuthero as a course of treatment lasting 4 to 5 weeks, on a daily basis. Usually a course of treatment suffices but long-term use is possible and without harmful side-effects.

These are just some of the many herbal remedies of Chinese herbal medicine. If you would like to visit a Chinese medical practitioner, please refer to the end of the chapter for details of the Register of Chinese Medical Herbalists.

Consulting A Herbalist

Western Medical Herbalists

A professional medical herbalist is trained to carry out a full medical examination in the same way as a GP, using the same type of equipment. Usually members of the National Institute of Medical Herbalists, these practitioners apply Western herbal medicine in a consulting room. Your blood pressure, pulse reading, blood and urine samples will all be taken.

A medical herbalist can give specialist advice on the use of herbal medicine for serious or long-term problems. At an initial consultation, a practitioner will ask you for details of your medical history, eating and exercise habits and whether stress is a factor in your daily life. As a result of the overall diagnosis, the herbalist will prescribe a single herb or combination of herbs and specify in which form the medicine is to be taken, such as a tincture, as pills or as infusions.

Finding A Practitioner

For a list of practitioners or further information write, enclosing a SAE to:

The National Institute of Medical Herbalists, 9 Palace Gate, Exeter EX1 1JA;

The General Council and Register of Consultant Herbalists, Marlborough House, Swanpool, Falmouth, Cornwall TR11 4HW.

Chinese Herbalists

Traditional Chinese herbalists tend to be confined to Chinese centres, practising mainly within the Chinese community. Write to the Register of Chinese Herbal Medicine, 138 Prestbury Road, Cheltenham GLS2 2DP, for information or a list of practitioners.

Ayurvedic And Unani Practitioners

Commonly known as *Vaids* and *Hakims*, these practitioners are mainly found within the Indian and Pakistani communities and offer treatment based on traditional principles.

Further Reading

A–Z of Modern Herbalism by Simon Mills (Diamond Books)
Herbal First Aid by Andrew Chevallier (Amberwood)
Herbal Medicine by Dian Dincin Buchman (Rider Books)
Herbalism : Headway Lifeguides by Francis Büning and Paul Hambly
   (Headway)
Thorsons' Guide to Medical Herbalism by David Hoffman (Thorsons)
Traditional Home Herbal Remedies by Jan de Vries (Mainstream
   Publishing)

5
HOMOEOPATHY: DEPENDENCE NO LONGER

The nature of addiction is first and foremost psychological. Homoeopathy is of relevance as it is a holistic therapy which tries to improve psychological and mental processes as well as physical processes; it aims to go beyond the mere alleviation of symptoms to address the actual causes of ill health. The ultimate aim of homoeopathic medicine is for the patient to reach such a level of health that there is no longer a need for, or dependence on, a medicine, a therapy or any other substance.

The principle on which homoeopathy is based is that 'Like cures like'. Homoeopaths consider that symptoms of a disease are a sign that the body is trying to heal itself. Modern medicine believes that if a person is ill, you cure the person by abolishing the symptoms. Conventional drugs are prescribed to ease the symptoms of a cold, a throat infection, a headache; homoeopathic medicine aims to enhance the self-healing mechanism of the body. If you want to cure a cold quickly, you should take yourself off to bed with a hot drink and try to sweat it out. Modern cold remedies, however, are designed to relieve, and suppress, symptoms such as high temperature and sweating.

Discovery Of Homoeopathy

A German doctor, Samuel Hahnemann, is credited with developing the theory and practice of modern homoeopathy and giving it its name during the early nineteenth century, but the principles of homoeopathy were already recognised by Hippocrates (400 BC) and supported by the renowned physician and philosopher Paracelsus in the fifteenth century. Paracelsus said that 'Those who merely study and treat the effects of disease are like those who imagine that they can drive away winter by brushing snow from the door. It is not the snow that causes the winter but the winter that causes the snow.'

Hahnemann was appalled by the way the conventional medicine of his day was being practised. He considered the customs of

bleeding patients, administering strong enemas and using powerful, and often dangerous (evidenced by the high patient death rate at the time), drugs to be both brutal and painful.

Hahnemann searched for a method of curing that was effective, safe and gentle. While translating Cullen's *Materia Medica,* he was puzzled by the explanation for the efficacy of cinchona bark in treating malaria. He proceeded to dose himself with cinchona bark for several days and developed malarial symptoms. In this way he established that, not only did cinchona bark alleviate the intermittent fever of malaria, but that large doses of it actually caused malarial symptoms in a normally healthy person.

Hahnemann went on to experiment with many other substances, testing them on himself, his family and friends. These experiments, called 'provings', involved the taking of very small doses of substances and carefully noting all the symptoms that were produced. Subsequently, patients suffering from similar symptoms were treated with the 'proven' drugs and the results were encouraging and often remarkable.

Hahnemann's research led him to criticise contemporary conventional medicine, especially the treatment of an illness with its opposite (*allopathic*) medicine. Instead, he argued, the remedy for the healing of the disease should be one that artificially produced symptoms as similar as possible to those produced by the disease itself.

The theory of homoeopathy developed, notwithstanding opposition from the orthodox medical profession. Homoeopathy's value was particularly highlighted in the European cholera epidemics when many lives were saved by a prescription of camphor suggested by Hahnemann. By the time of Hahnemann's death in 1843, homoeopathy had spread over most of continental Europe and had penetrated Russia, South America, Great Britain and parts of the USA.

How Homoeopathy Works

The fundamental difference between homoeopathic and allopathic medicine lies in the way in which symptoms are viewed. While allopathic medicine views symptoms as being part of the disease, a homoeopath regards them as an adaptive response by the body in defending itself: the symptoms are evidence of the body's attempts to heal itself. The homoeopath's task is to prescribe a remedy that

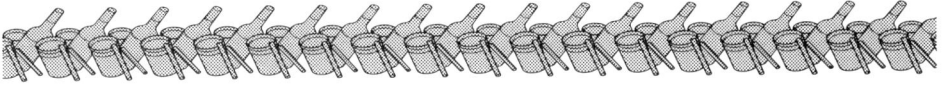

will stimulate the body to heal itself more quickly. The correct remedy is one that will create symptoms similar to those of the disease process.

Homoeopathy is based on the following three principles:

The Law Of Similars

The human organism is believed to have a great capacity to heal itself and is in a constant state of self-repair. The homoeopath prescribes a remedy which, through previous 'provings' on healthy people and from clinical observations, is known to produce a similar symptom picture to that of the patient. The prescribed remedy then stimulates and assists the body's own natural healing efforts.

The Single Remedy

Homoeopaths believe that the body should only be stimulated by a single remedy at any one time. It is the patient's whole system which is out of balance even though there may be a multiplicity of symptoms, which may not appear to be connected. The single remedy allows the homoeopath clearly to observe and evaluate its effect before further prescription is considered.

The Minimal Dose

Only a minute dose, in the form of a specially prepared potency, is needed, since the patient is highly sensitive to its stimulus. This is because of the similarity between the remedy's known symptom picture and that of the patient. The specific potency and number of doses are determined by the homoeopath, according to the needs of the individual.

Much debate and controversy surrounds the concept of dilution. As homoeopathic remedies are diluted to such an extent, sceptics say that it is inconceivable that any of the original substance is left at all, so how can such a remedy work? Homoeopaths would argue that, although they do not yet understand the mechanism, there is ample evidence that it does work.

Among the wide range of theories put forward to explain how homoeopathy works, one is the suggestion that looking for a physical explanation ignores the holistic nature of the therapy.

Rather, it may well be the case that the high potencies may be acting at a very subtle level of energy and that these remedies vibrate or resonate with a person's 'vital force'. The right homoeopathic remedy is like a boost of subtle energy which returns the body to its optimum frequency and so aids recovery. Once the body is in tune, resonating at its appropriate rate, it is able to use its immune system to throw off the negative stimuli that cause illness.

A clinical trial, conducted in Glasgow in 1978, compared three groups of patients with rheumatoid arthritis. One group was told to take aspirin, another group a *placebo* (a non-medicated substance) and the last group homoeopathic remedies. A year after the commencement of the trial, the condition in the homoeopathic group was more significantly improved than in the two other groups.

Other trials conducted since then include David Reilly and Morag Taylor's hay fever trial in 1985, and Peter Fisher's fibrositis trial in 1986. In both of these, homoeopathic remedies were found to have a demonstrable effect in relieving symptoms. A recent study of over 100 clinical trials showed about 80 positive in favour of homoeopathy.

Homoeopathic Medicines

The range of sources for homoeopathic medicines is immense, since they can be prepared from anything that causes symptoms. This includes plant, animal and mineral matter, extracts of chemical compounds and bacterial products. Today there are over 2,500 substances that have been prepared for homoeopathic medicines, from belladonna (deadly nightshade) and aconite (monkshood) to lachesis (extract of snake venom) and cantharis (derived from Spanish fly).

The medicines are made up by taking the raw material through a process of serial dilution and *succussion* (vigorous shaking). Each stage of succussion increases the potency which is given a number and a letter. Potencies with an 'X' affix are diluted 1:9 and those with a 'C' affix are diluted 1:99 at each successive stage. Plant materials are instantly soluble, but minerals and metals need to undergo a process called *trituration* (grinding) with a milk/sugar powder up to the 3X potency before they become soluble; at that point the dilution and succussion process continues in the same manner as plants.

Taking The Medicines

These are prescribed according to the needs and vitality of the patient and also to the level of vitality of the disease process of the patient. The potency has to be similar to the disease process resonance, as well as similar to the symptom picture. (The lower potencies are those which have been subjected to less dilution than the higher ones.) Today there are many outlets which sell homoeopathic medicines over the counter, such as health food stores and pharmacies. Preparations are available in tablet form, granules, *pillules* (small pills), powders or as a liquid, and creams, ointments and lotions for external use. It is usual for over-the-counter remedies to be of a lower potency, either 6C or 30C – caution is advised in the repetition of the 30C, as this is a relatively high potency. Higher potency medicines are generally recommended for use only by experienced and qualified homoeopaths.

The same medicine may be administered in different ways, perhaps a single dose in a high-potency form or a low dose repeated frequently. The choice of method depends on the nature of the illness and the individual needs of the patient. For example, if a person has been ill for a long time and the body is in physical disrepair, one way to take the homoeopathic medicine would be in repeated doses in a lower potency, to stimulate the immune system. However, a healthier person may just need a single high-potency remedy for a response.

As dilution lessens the toxic effects of the substance used, this contrasts markedly with the powerful drugs often used in allopathic medicine, a number of which have been known to produce alarming side-effects. Further, since conventional drugs are prescribed for their individual capacities to work upon specific parts of the body, it follows that several different drugs might be prescribed to treat the various symptoms of one individual. The effects of such combinations are often unknown or not recognised.

A homoeopath, however, prescribes a single medicine in an appropriate potency which will stimulate a person's immune or defence mechanism and bring about an improvement in general health.

A Visit To A Homoeopath

Be prepared to answer a lot of questions when you visit a professional homoeopath. Each symptom will need to be described

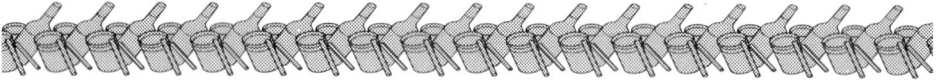

in terms of you and your general lifestyle, when the condition commenced, its sensation – whether the pain is dull, sharp, continuous, etc. – when it occurs or is worse, and what it feels better for. On the basis of this information as a whole, the practitioner will analyse the details that make up your case in order to select the homoeopathic remedy that will match your presenting symptoms more precisely. If treatment is not successful, another remedy will be prescribed. The same remedy may be administered in different ways, depending on your particular needs.

Homoeopathy For Addictions

It is important to note that homoeopaths consider health and well-being as the experience of freedom on physical, emotional and mental levels. As well as treating physical ailments, homoeopathy can be used to help emotional and psychological problems, such as addictions, phobias or obsessive behaviour.

Homoeopaths are trained to observe and make sense of information that is given about an individual's state of physical, mental and emotional health. From analysis of this information, a pattern emerges which suggests to the homoeopath that a particular remedy will be of value in establishing the necessary impetus for a cure. Case analysis consists of a careful selection of the symptoms that convey the individual nature of the patient's case on all three levels, and the matching of these symptoms with the homoeopathic remedy which provides the closest fit. In the process of this selection, psychological and emotional symptoms are often given high priority, especially where there is a marked disturbance on these levels.

Homoeopaths will often speak of different constitutional types, in other words, individuals who show characteristics on physical and emotional levels that fit into certain predictable patterns. They may often be described as broadly 'arsenicum', 'phosphorus', 'pulsatilla', 'nux vomica' or 'sulphur' type. If we take the example of someone who shows strong characteristics of the nux vomica type, they are likely to be impatient, irritable, hurried, intolerant, impulsive and inclined to workaholism. They often experience problems as a result of 'living in the fast lane' and may resort to stimulants, alcohol, cigarettes and drugs in order to keep going while under pressure. As a result, problems such as constipation (often from overuse of painkillers or a fast-food diet), indigestion and tension headaches

might arise. Patients who respond well to nux vomica will often demonstrate symptoms of this nature when overstressed or under the weather. However, it is important to emphasise that this is a flexible, fluid system, with most individuals demonstrating characteristics of a range of remedies within their broad constitutional type. These can vary in response to changes in the physical and emotional environment, diet, stress or bereavement.

Although homoeopathy is of value in helping problems of addiction, it must be stressed that help of this nature should ideally be sought from a qualified homoeopath who will have the necessary experience and objectivity to deal with any complications that may arise during the course of treatment. This is especially true of situations where addiction is of drug dependence, since medication should not be discontinued abruptly, or without appropriate medical supervision or support. It is for this reason that no mention of specific remedies has been made in this chapter.

A Conversation With A Homoeopathic Practitioner

Q. What are the goals of homoeopathic treatment?
A. The goal is to get you to a level of health, balance and freedom from limitations so that you eventually need only very infrequent medication.

Q. Why do homoeopaths ask so many questions?
A. Homoeopathy does not treat specific diseases as such, but treats individuals. Hence a detailed understanding of the patient is fundamental to making a correct prescription.

The homoeopath must attempt an almost impossible task – that of coming quickly to a complete understanding of an individual. The questioning process is essential for forming and developing this understanding.

The homoeopath needs to be an acute listener and observer – our job is primarily to get your symptom picture and to match this to a remedy. So we want to hear your story and listen sympathetically, without making any value judgements, and match this information to the right remedy.

To match a remedy to an individual we must know all the person's limitations clearly: this includes mental, emotional and physical levels, and such aspects as general energy, effects of environment and causative factors.

Q. How many appointments are necessary?

A. In the beginning, that is, in the first six months, visits may be more frequent and will taper off as you become healthier. We feel we need to see you at first more frequently (follow-ups are usually every four to six weeks in the beginning) to work with you and evaluate your progress. Yet we are not insensitive to the cost of treatment and do not wish to make this a burden.

If a remedy has acted curatively, even in deep and complex cases, after the initial follow-up we may not need to see you for some time. This is because the remedy has brought your system into balance and, in our experience, this state can last for a long time. We also need to wait until the next 'remedy picture' comes up clearly. This is the time to have renewed faith in your body's healing abilities.

Q. How can I be involved?

A. You don't have to believe in homoeopathic remedies in order for them to work (we treat babies and there are homoeopathic vets). But to select the correct remedy and for the treatment to continue to act, your cooperation and commitment is necessary.
You can help by:

- Noting any changes after you take the remedy – keeping a weekly journal can be helpful for bringing to your follow-up consultations. Please note general changes as well as specific ones.
- Giving a clear and complete account of your symptoms on all levels.
- Above all, communicating any concerns or questions you may have. We are always trying to find better ways of helping you and welcome your comments.

Q. How long does treatment take?

A. This is a difficult question to answer, but after several interviews the homoeopath is better able to give you an idea of this. In simpler problems and in acute situations results can begin quickly and dramatically.

For a small percentage of very healthy individuals one or two treatments may be all that is needed to stabilise the system for years at a stretch but such an ideal would, for most people, be an unrealistic expectation.

Q. Should I come back after I am feeling better?

A. The four to six week follow-up is important to return for. After you are feeling consistently better we would like to see you for regular check-ups to prevent future problems. Usually this is at four to six month intervals.

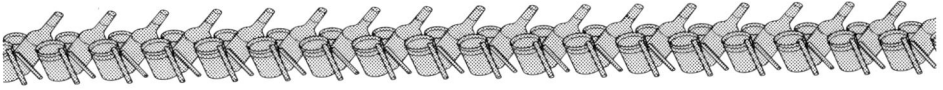

Q. How can a few doses do anything or last a long time?

A. The remedies are highly potent – they are prepared in what is called a 'potentised dilution' and dropped on to tiny lactose granules, pilules, tablets or powders, or can be taken in liquid form. They simply catalyse or trigger a response by the body on an energetic level, rather than effect chemical change. So, ultimately, what works better after the remedy is taken is your own regulating system. The remedy helps the body develop a natural, positive momentum which continues to gain strength and eliminate disease.

Q. Can homoeopathy work in more complex or chronic cases, and how long does it take?

A. In more complex cases homoeopathic treatment is like peeling away the layers of an onion. Briefly, this means that we build up layers of symptoms, or 'pathology' as a response to certain stresses as we go through in life. These 'layers' are laid down and can be 'peeled' away effectively with homoeopathic remedies. During treatment old sets of symptoms may come up (but because with each successive remedy you are healthier they will not be as severe as in the past). A recurrence of an old set of symptoms may be the indication for a new remedy to be given. Even some hereditary tendencies can be eliminated with homoeopathy.

So in deep or chronic problems the curative process may be gradual and consultations more frequent.

Q. What happens if the symptoms seem to return?

A. If you had a good curative response to a remedy and then after, say, two to six months (or at any time) a relapse seems to occur, we usually recommend waiting a few days to see if your system re-balances itself. If any severe symptoms develop, do not wait. If the symptoms persist after a week, then a repeat of the remedy may be necessary. If so, another appointment would be needed.

Do not get disappointed or discouraged at this point and feel that homoeopathy is not working for you – this is just a phase of getting you to a consistently good state of health.

This situation may mean a new remedy is indicated as a 'layer' of symptoms from the past comes up and needs to be treated.

Q. What will interfere with the remedy working?

A. Camphor products and highly aromatic essential oils, such as peppermint and menthol can all interfere. There are certain therapies that can interfere, such as chemical therapies (natural or otherwise), high-potency vitamins, very intensive exercise programmes, and certain

dental procedures. It is not usually a good idea to have acupuncture during a course of homoeopathic treatment as it interferes with the 'vital force' and both treatments are based on the premise that they work by stimulating the body's healing powers.

We have found that massage, mild chiropractic and osteopathic treatments and certain gentle therapies or medications do not interfere with homoeopathy.

If you are considering any other therapy, consult your homoeopath first.

It is also best to avoid, or at least greatly reduce, the intake of stimulants such as coffee and other caffeine drinks.

Q. What about seeing a GP?

A. Homoeopathy is complementary to the health care that is available. We recommend that you should maintain your relationship with your doctor, especially for routine needs and emergencies. Your GP will also arrange for you to have any blood tests or X-rays, etc. or refer you to a consultant.

Finding A Practitioner

An increasing number of qualified medical doctors now offer homoeopathic treatment. Most of them have taken a postgraduate training course to become a Member or a Fellow of the Faculty of Homoeopathy (MSHom or FFHom). A register of practitioners is maintained by the Faculty of Homoeopathy, c/o the Royal London Homoeopathic Hospital, Great Ormond Street, London WC1N 3HR. Many of the professional homoeopaths have trained for four years at accredited colleges and have become graduate or registered members of the Society of Homoeopaths (RSHom). For a list of registered homoeopaths, write to The Society of Homoeopaths, 2 Artizan Road, Northampton NN1 4HU.

In addition to the private and NHS practitioners there are five NHS homoeopathic hospitals, in London, Bristol, Tunbridge Wells, Liverpool and Glasgow. There are also a number of private clinics nationally. Further information may be obtained from The British Homoeopathic Association, 27A Devonshire Street, London W1N 1RJ.

Further Reading

Everybody's Guide to Homoeopathic Medicines by Stephen Cummings
   and Dana Ullman (Gollancz)
Homoeopathy for Emergencies by Phyllis Speight (C W Daniels)
Homoeopathy: Headway Lifeguides by Beth MacEoin (Headway)
Homoeopathy, Medicine for the New Man by George Vithoulkas
   (Thorsons)
Homoeopathy: Medicine for the 21st Century by Dana Ullman
   (Thorsons)
The Complete Homoeopathy Handbook: A Guide to Everyday Health Care
   by Miranda Castro (Macmillan)
The Family Guide to Homoeopathy: The Safe Form of Medicine for the Future
   by Andrew Lockie (Elm Tree Books)

6

ANTHROPOSOPHICAL MEDICINE: SPIRITUAL FREEDOM FROM DEPENDENCY

Orthodox medicine is based upon hypothesis and experimentation; if something cannot be proven by experiment, it does not exist as a scientific fact. This premise can lead to an oversimplification, if it is applied to the physical aspect of existence only. Indeed, in conventional medicine (based on natural science) this simplification is a fundamental tenet, and we call it *reductionism*. All aspects of our existence – the physical, the manifestations of living organisms, the emotional and mental or spiritual aspects – are reduced to mere expressions of the physical.

In anthroposophical medicine, the methods and discipline of (natural) science are applied to other, non-physical levels of reality. Anthroposophy is also called a spiritual science; it acknowledges the other levels of our existence and investigates their inter-relationships. This approach broadens the possibilities of treatment of illness.

Anthroposophy was founded by the Austrian philosopher and scientist Rudolf Steiner (1861– 1925); he outlined the philosophical foundations of his ideas in his treatise *The Philosophy of Freedom*. Steiner describes in this, and other works, how the human being has not just a body, but also a soul and spirit. He discerns four aspects to the bodily nature of the human being; health and well-being depends on a harmonious working together of these aspects.

Together with a Dutch doctor, Ita Wegman, Steiner further developed his ideas for medicine, and they wrote the book which marked the beginning of anthroposophical medicine: *The Fundamentals of Therapy*.

The Four Aspects Of The Human Being

In addition to the physical body, three other elements are present in the human body which complete the picture of the human being. In

anthroposophical terms they are called the *etheric* (or life-)body, the *astral* (or sentient-) body and the *ego* (-body). These elements are common to us all, but cannot be perceived directly by the ordinary physical senses. Essentially the *etheric* body is concerned with growth, repair and replenishment, the *astral* body represents the sentient and emotional life, and the *ego* embodies the individual spiritual core, which man alone possesses.

The Etheric Body

This is the force which governs the existence of the physical body. It imbues the physical body with life, without which the physical body deteriorates and disintegrates; this happens naturally after death, when only physical laws govern. The etheric body is responsible for keeping the physical parts of the body into a whole and maintaining its integrity by continuous repair and restructuring. It is the very source of our natural tendency to heal and recover from less serious ailments, without additional medical help. In short, the etheric body constantly guards against death and decay (physical laws).

The Astral Body

The astral body represents the soul element, common to animals and humans, and differentiates them from the plants and minerals. Our sentient being, consciousness as such, is carried by the astral body.

It is through our sentient (astral) body, that we are aware of emotions, feelings, thoughts: a level which cannot be measured tangibly, but is very much a reality. A conventional doctor believes that this aspect of our existence is a mere manifestation of physical and chemical processes. An anthroposophical practitioner regards the sentient life and therefore the sentient (or astral) body as a reality, just as much as the physical.

The astral body has, generally speaking, a strong *catabolic* (breaking down) effect in the human body, and so has an opposite effect to the etheric body, which is constantly endeavouring to build and repair. So, good health prevails for as long as the destructive (*catabolic*) processes, due to the activity of the astral body, are held in check and in equilibrium by the building (*anabolic*) activity of the etheric body. An imbalance between the two will result in illness.

The Ego

Present only in the human being, the ego adds an additional level of consciousness, namely the self-consciousness. It comprises the ability to think independently and brings an awareness of being autonomous. So humans are able to refrain from instinctive behaviour, if reasoning leads them: a quality that is not present in the animal world. The human ability to learn, develop and become an independent and lonely being, is due to the ego, the spiritual core of man. On a bodily level, this ego has quite a complicated task and influences, generally speaking, the etheric body in an anabolic way and joins the astral body in its catabolic activity. However, the ego always guards the totality of the bodily processes and works mainly through the warmth organisation of the body.

The Anthroposophical View of Illness

Anthroposophical practitioners look at health and illness in terms of the interrelationships between the ego, the astral body, the etheric body and the physical body. These four aspects of the human being interrelate and interconnect to each other in different parts of the body and its organ systems.

The three main functional organ systems within anthroposophical medical thought are described as the nerve–sense system, the metabolic limb system and the rhythmical system.

The nerve–sense system comprises, physically, the central nervous system (brain, sense organs, spinal cord) and the whole of the autonomous nervous system (connecting to all the internal organs).

This organ system lacks vitality, regeneration and movement. The nervous system is very vulnerable and easily damaged if deprived of oxygen and other nutrients. The life-bringing activity of the etheric body is therefore very minimal, and the catabolic action of the astral body dominates, bringing about consciousness, thought and perception.

In the metabolic limb system we find a wealth of vital activity in the main digestive organs (liver, pancreas, stomach etc.), the lymphatic system and our reproductive organs. The muscles of our limbs are the main consumers of nutrients and are full of life and movement.

There is no consciousness in this system and we are not aware of its anabolic processes, unless there is something wrong and we feel

pain; pain is heightened consciousness, and is experienced through our astral or sentient body. The astral body also works in the metabolic limb system, but here not in a catabolic way. It serves the predominantly anabolic activity of the etheric body. Whilst in the nerve–sense system the catabolic activity overrules the anabolic.

The tension between the catabolic and anabolic processes in these two organ systems is regulated by a third functional activity–that of the rhythmical system.

The Three Systems In Anthroposophical Medicine			
Nerve–Sense:	Thinking	Conscious	Cooling Catabolic Hardening
Rhythmic:	Feeling	Dream-like	Balancing Mediating
Metabolic Limb:	Volition	Unconscious	Warming Anabolic Softening

This rhythmical system of the body is found most clearly in the rhythmical activity of the heart, circulation and breathing: *systole* (contraction) and *diastole* (expansion), in-breath and out-breathing, illustrate the constantly changing balance of the rhythmical system. It incorporates and balances both the primarily catabolic action of the nerve–sense system (contraction, consciousness enhancing), and the mainly anabolic activity of the metabolic limb system (relaxation, regeneration).

Such a dynamic and artistic view of the functions of the human body enables the anthroposophical doctor to relate anatomical and physiological aspects to psychological and spiritual aspects in the human being. Illness and dis-ease result from imbalances in the interrelating systems. Such an understanding broadens the scope of diagnosis as well as treatment. Different methods of treatment are used to achieve this.

The Medicines

When and where appropriate and/or necessary, conventional medicines are and will be used. However, the remedies developed in anthroposophical medicine are derived from plant or mineral and, occasionally, animal sources. The choice of substance is based on

the perceived relationship between the life process in the human body and nature. Steiner gave many indications of how certain substances relate to bodily processes and organs; for example, he indicated how the seven metals (lead, tin, iron, copper, mercury, silver and gold) correspond to organs and organ-processes. So an anthroposophical practitioner might prescribe a potentised preparation of tin, as drops or in the form of an ointment, for a patient with liver problems, or copper for regulation of the kidney function. Plant substances may well be given in material doses, as well as in potentised form.

Artistic Therapies

Artistic activity engages and appeals to the creative sources of the human being; the aim in therapy would be to mobilise such creative potential, and not particularly to create a work of art as such. Being engaged in a creative process also influences our bodily functions, in different and often subtle ways. Painting with a blue colour only will have a calming effect on our breathing and circulation, whilst sculpture work will engage our will more directly. For both physiological and psychological reasons, activities such as music, painting, form-drawing and sculpture may be recommended as part of an integral treatment plan.

Eurythmy Therapy

This therapy developed out of the art-form *eurythmy*, which Steiner also called *visible speech* or *visible music*. It is an art of movement (dance) through which the formative and creative forces of the world are made visible, in an artistic way. The eurythmy therapist uses specific gestures that express, for instance, certain vowels or consonants in a certain sequence. Through these movements, a soul-mood is created and they engender changes in the breathing, circulation and distribution of muscular tension. The exercises are used in the treatment of both physical and psychological disorders.

Hydrotherapy And Massage

In these treatments, the physical body is more directly addressed. A special form of rhythmical massage was developed, which in comparison with other forms of massage, is quite gentle. The masseur will identify patterns of muscular tension, warmth

penetration and distribution, and the tone of the skin and underlying soft tissues. Particularly the irregularities of the warmth organisation are noted, as the warmth as such is regarded as the physical medium through which the activity of the ego works. Through addressing the warmth, with oil-dispersion baths and using particular aromatic oils in the massage itself, a self-sustaining improvement and redistribution of warmth and tension can be achieved. Particularly the rhythmical system is strengthened in relation to the other functional systems; the breathing relaxes and deepens, a healthier flow of warmth comes about, relieving inappropriate tensions.

The Treatment Of Addictions

It will be clear from the above considerations that quite different approaches to the treatment of psychiatric and psychosomatic conditions are available out of anthroposophical medicine. The spiritual dimension (ego) of man can, as such, never be ill, but its strivings and intentions may well be obscured and deformed, by the deforming effects of the functions of the astral and etheric activities in the body and its organs (processes). In anthroposophical psychiatry, a relationship has been found between certain organ processes and soul conditions. So, for instance, depressive moods and overt depressive illnesses are attributed to liver processes; the mainly anabolic (up building) chemistry of the liver, gives the soul a depth of feeling which can be exaggerated and result in depression. Compulsive and obsessional traits of the personality are due to a too strong influence of the lung physiology upon the soul life. Fear and anxiety conditions can be related to the activity of the kidneys and adrenal glands (adrenaline!).

In the case of substance abuse/addiction, usually both bodily and pyschological health are profoundly affected and need addressing. Deeply engrained psychological and physiological habits have formed, that are geared to gratify the need for a sense of self, a sense of well-being; anything that quenches this thirst for a sense of self and thereby takes away the painful emptiness, can become an addiction. Essentially, all addictions originate out of thirst for spiritual and soul development, i.e. out of the ego of man that itself can never be ill.

The starting point for treatment of any addiction will have to take account of this spiritual/developmental dimension. Awakening this positive will for development is crucial; without this 'good will for the

spirit', no cure works for longer than the supervised phase of treatment. Counselling and intensive artistic work (painting, eurythmy, sculpture etc.) are included in any treatment programme. Usually relationship and community building activities are needed to foster development.

Every addictive substance leads to damage, much greater than is commonly thought. This damage occurs on the one hand in the physical and etheric sphere, and on the other hand in the inability of the ego to master and provide guidance in life. A range of anthroposophical medicines, combined initially with therapeutic massage, will address the damage of the bodily functions. The expertise of an anthroposophical doctor is needed to assess each patient's medicinal and therapeutic requirements.

Finding A Practitioner

Anthroposophical practitioners are all qualified medical doctors who have taken a further postgraduate course recognised by the Anthroposophical Medical Association in Britain. Some may be found working in the NHS, although others work privately or in the Rudolf Steiner schools and homes for children in need of special care (Camphill Communities). Residential treatment is also available.

Consultations are very much like seeing a GP except that there may be additional details and questions about, for example, lifestyle and emotional situation. Diagnosis is made in the same way as a GP and treatment is prescribed depending on the individual characteristics of the patient.

Treatment will range from conventional, anthroposophical or herbal to homoeopathic types of medication. In addition, eurythmy, massage, hydrotherapy or an art therapy may be prescribed to complement and enhance the treatment.

The Anthroposophical Medical Association maintains a register of members. It is based at the Park Attwood Therapeutic Centre, Trimpley, Bewdley, Worcestershire DY12 1RE.

Further Reading

Anthroposophical Medicine by Dr M Evans and I Rodger (Thorsons)
Anthroposophical Medicine and its Remedies by Otto Wolf (Weleda Ag)
Rudolf Steiner: Scientist of the Invisible by A P Shepherd (Floris Books)

7

AROMATHERAPY: SCENTS OF SUPPORT

People who are trying to break free from an addiction need a great deal of encouragement and support: *physical support*, since their addiction has damaged their health and weakened their body – weaning off the addictive substance is a further, albeit short-term, strain on the body; *emotional support*, because most addictions are an emotional prop and the addict needs to find reassurance from other sources; *mental support*, because the addiction leaves the addict psychologically dependent on the addictive substance and perhaps with little faith that the addiction can be overcome.

The human body has five senses: sight, hearing, touch, taste and smell. Aromatherapy uses the power of scent, or aroma, to heal the body, mind and spirit. Think of your reaction to the smell of freshly cut grass on a summer's day, or to bread baking; and your opposite reaction to the smell of a sewage farm, or the smell of somebody's bad breath! We spend millions of pounds each year on products which make our homes and our bodies smell nice. The perfume industry thrives on our wish to smell desirable. Different odours evoke different sensations, memories, images. Exactly why is not completely understood, but the answer may lie in the fact that the area of the brain which is sensitive to smell is close to the area which deals with emotions, memory and intuition (the *limbic* area).

Aromatherapy is doubly beneficial since it combines the healing effect of aroma with the therapeutic effect of massage. Not only does this enable physical concentration on specific problem areas, it also relaxes and eases stress. Touch is an important medium to communicate love. A hug makes us feel loved and secure. As babies and young children touch was a vital part of our everyday lives and made us feel cared for and special. Massage relaxes the mind and tones the body.

The Ancient Art Of Aromatherapy

Aromatherapy is not a new concept. The power of scent has been known since ancient times. The Egyptians used aromatherapy in

embalming, the Romans were skilled users of plant essences and it is thought that the knights of the Holy Crusade brought back the knowledge and use of aromatic oils to this country as a result of their travels to the East. But it is an Arab physician, Avicenna, who is credited with developing the use of aromatic oils in healing and perfected their distillation. The methods have remained virtually the same 900 years after his death.

The nineteenth century saw a shift from plant-based remedies to synthetic drugs in this country but this century has seen a revival in the use of aromatic oils as healers. Professor René Gattefosse pioneered the rediscovery of aromatherapy purely by chance: accidentally burning his hand, he plunged it into the nearest available liquid, which happened to be lavender essential oil. Surprised at how quickly his hand healed, and without leaving any scar, he investigated further the power of aromatic oils. He went on to develop treatments which were used during the First World War. Today the shift back to natural remedies has seen an upsurge in the interest and practice of aromatherapy.

Extracting The Oils

Plants and herbs all contain essential oils, some of which are used for fragrance, in cooking or as medicinal remedies. Oil can be extracted from any part of the plant, the leaf, flower or seeds, and steam distillation is the most common method of extraction. Pressurised steam is passed through the plant and the heat releases the oil which evaporates and condenses and is then collected. A recent innovation uses vacuum distillation: the lower temperatures required preserve the delicate oils more successfully. The essential oils of citrus come from the fruit's rind, and this is extracted by pressure to the rind itself, a technique known as *expression.*

The oils contain as many as 100 different substances which interact to give their full benefit: for this reason chemical synthesisation of oils is neither effective nor feasible. When you are purchasing essential oils, ensure that they are genuine pure essential oils, in order to experience the full benefit of aromatherapy.

You should only buy oils that come in tightly sealed, dark glass bottles. The oils sold in clear plastic bottles in some high street stores have little aromatherapeutic value, because light can break down important components of the oils. At home they should also be kept stored in dark glass bottles (green or brown or blue) in cool conditions, although not in the refrigerator.

Steam and essential oil

Condenser

Flowers

Essential oil

Perfumed
water

Steam

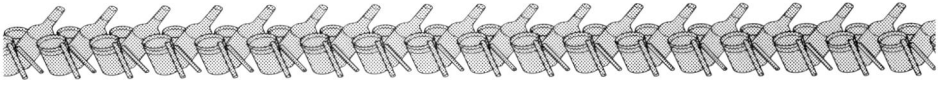

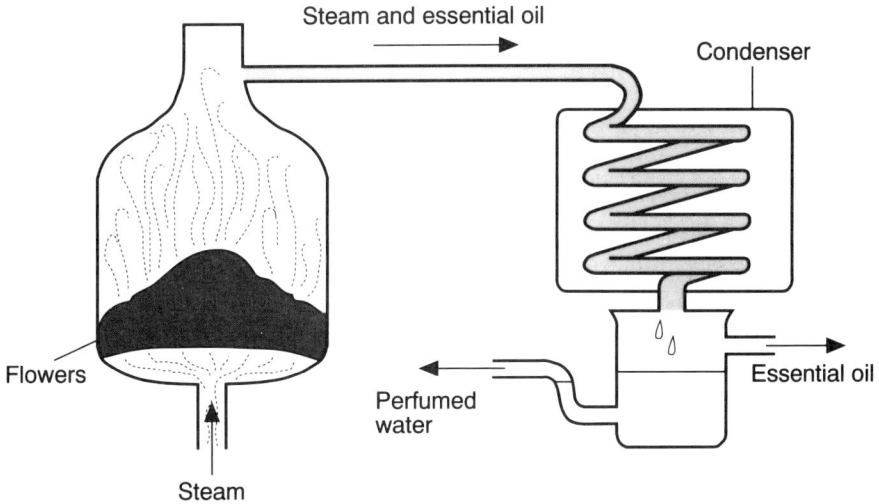

Steam distillation process

Administering Essential Oils

Aromatherapy employs three different methods of administering
the oils. The most potent is by inhalation. A few drops are placed on
a handkerchief and inhaled, taking deep breaths. The oils pass
directly into the system via the brain and thence throughout the
body. Another method is by adding a few drops of the essential oil
to the bath, combining the dual effects of the oil itself with the
naturally relaxing effects of water on the body. The third method
combines with the benefit of massage, when the essential oils are
added to a carrier oil (almond or sunflower seed oil, for example)
and rubbed into the body. The oils pass into the bloodstream via the
skin and then act on the body.

Aromatherapy: At Home And Visiting A Practitioner

A professional aromatherapist holds a qualification in aromatherapy
and will have general medical knowledge in order to suggest the
correct therapy and oil. A visit to a practitioner will start with an
overall examination of your general state of health, and include
enquiries into your lifestyle and your particular addiction. Muscle

testing and reflexology (the therapy of foot massage, see page 103) are sometimes employed to establish any problem areas which you may not have identified.

A specific, tailor-made 'prescription' will be prepared for you, taking into account your own likes and dislikes of scents. A course of treatment is typically six sessions, although obviously more may be required. The professional aromatherapist will be able to administer healing massage to stimulate areas which are in need and to relax other parts of the body which require stress relief.

Your aromatherapist may recommend that you continue the treatment at home. Foot and hand baths, as well as ordinary baths, are obvious home treatments. You may be prescribed a compress, which is basically essential oil dripped on to an absorbent material and secured with a bandage. The compress is usually left on for a couple of hours. A few drops of essential oil on dry flowers to give room scent may be advised or, if you are able to go to a sauna, some drops placed on the hot coals. In these various ways your treatment will be extended outside the sessions with the aromatherapist.

Massage Techniques

What can you expect from an aromatherapist when it comes to massage? Well, to begin with the surroundings will be conducive to relaxation. That means that a special room will be set aside purely for massage. It will be well ventilated and very warm – no-one can relax if they are physically cold. Pastel shades will help to create a calm atmosphere and there may be flowers in the room. A purpose-built massage couch ensures the optimum comfort. A small amount of oil is placed in a dish (the oil is never poured directly onto the skin) and then rubbed into the masseur's hands. The spine, limbs and face will be worked on, although not the eyes as the eye tissue is very delicate and would be irritated. Particular attention is given to promoting an overall feeling of relaxation, as kicking an addiction inevitably raises stress levels which, unless they are relieved, will push you back into your addiction.

Additionally, attention is given to particular parts of the body which have been under stress from your addiction: the liver and digestive system if alcohol is your problem, the stomach if it is caffeine to which you are addicted, the respiratory system if you are giving up smoking, and the whole body if you are trying to come off cocaine, heroin, tranquillisers or sugar.

Essential Oils Used In The Treatment Of Addictions

For All Addictions

While you are giving up your addiction there are several essential oils which can support you emotionally and physically. Some of the essential oils listed can be hazardous in pregnancy. If you are pregnant, please consult a qualified aromatherapist before proceeding with self-treatment.

- To counter depression, bergamot, chamomile, geranium, lavender, patchouli, rose, sandalwood, and ylang ylang are all effective.
- To raise your spirits, clary sage and jasmine are beneficial.
- Nervous tension can be eased with basil, marjoram, neroli, rose and tangerine.
- Chamomile, cypress, lavender and thyme will ease irritability.
- Insomnia will respond to chamomile, marjoram, rose and ylang ylang.
- Ginger and jasmine raise confidence levels, while benzoin is said to ease loneliness.
- If indecision is a problem, a typical side-effect of coming off tranquillisers or the hard drugs, basil and patchouli are beneficial.
- The immune system can be boosted with chamomile, lemon and thyme.

For Alcohol Problems

- In addition to the general herbs listed above, fennel is beneficial for alcoholism. Fennel smells like aniseed and is quite pungent. It detoxifies, eliminates fluids and soothes a troubled digestive system. It can be used in a bath, a massage or as a compress.
- Ylang ylang, one of the generally beneficial herbs listed above, will also help to steady an irregular heartbeat, and can be inhaled, bathed in or used as a compress, diffuser or in a massage.
- Tangerine, chamomile, geranium, lemon, peppermint, rose and rosemary are all effective tonics for the liver.
- Loss of appetite is improved with bergamot, black pepper, chamomile, fennel, ginger and juniper.

For Caffeine Addiction

- In addition to the general oils beneficial to all addictions, the stomach pains which excess caffeine often produce can be eased with chamomile, ginger, marjoram, peppermint and rosemary.
- Mental fatigue and inability to concentrate, the reasons why most of us turn to caffeine, will dissipate with basil, peppermint and rosemary.

For Heroin Addiction

- In addition to the generally beneficial oils for addictions, lavender, lemongrass and rosemary will improve wasted muscle tone.
- Exhaustion responds well to benzoin, juniper, lavender and thyme.
- Jasmine and juniper diminish pessimism; basil, ginger and thyme improve poor memory.
- Coldness and shivers are improved with benzoin, black pepper, cypress and rose.
- Stomach pains need the beneficial effects of chamomile, fennel, ginger, lavender, marjoram, peppermint and rosemary.
- Nausea and vomiting ease with basil, chamomile, fennel, lavender and peppermint.

For Cocaine Addiction

- The main effects of cocaine withdrawal being pessimism, loneliness, lack of self-confidence, fearfulness, hysteria and panic, the general oils listed for addictions form the main treatment for cocaine withdrawal (see 'For All Addictions' on page 95).
- High blood pressure can be treated with chamomile, lavender, lemon, marjoram, neroli and ylang ylang.
- Sinusitis responds to cajeput, eucalyptus, lavender, lemon, tea-tree and thyme.

For Nicotine Addiction

- As well as the general list of essential oils for addictions, nicotine withdrawal will be easier with specific oils aimed at calming the nervous system. Such oils are basil, cypress, marjoram, neroli, patchouli, rose, sandalwood and tangerine.
- Oversensitivity will respond to chamomile, cypress, geranium and lavender.

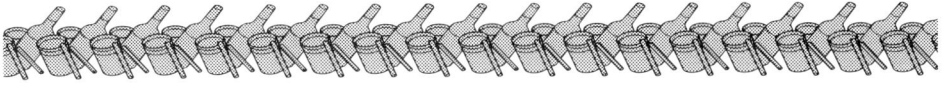

- Mood swings will benefit from chamomile, geranium and lavender.
- Lack of concentration will improve with basil, peppermint and rosemary.
- Anger is eased by chamomile and ylang ylang, while panic and hysteria are calmed by chamomile, clary sage, neroli and lavender.
- Shortness of breath will respond to fennel, frankincense and lavender.
- Poor circulation benefits from benzoin, black pepper, cypress, ginger, lemon, tangerine and thyme.

For Sugar Addiction

- In addition to the general oils listed for all addictions, sugar withdrawal will benefit from chamomile, geranium and lavender for mood swings.
- Diabetes responds to eucalyptus, geranium and juniper.
- For women, thrush (caused by the yeast-like fungus *Candida albicans*) is improved with bergamot, lemon, myrrh and tea-tree.

For Tranquilliser Addiction

- In addition to the general oils listed for all addictions, and depending on the type of tranquilliser from which you are withdrawing, the following may be useful:
- For constipation, black pepper, fennel, marjoram, rose and rosemary.
- For diarrhoea, black pepper, cajeput, chamomile, cypress, eucalyptus, geranium, ginger, lavender, lemon, myrrh, neroli, peppermint, rosemary and sandalwood.
- A generally sluggish digestion will improve with black pepper, fennel and peppermint.
- Stomach ulcers can be relieved with chamomile, fennel, ginger, lavender, marjoram, peppermint and rosemary.
- Hysteria and panic benefit from chamomile, clary sage, lavender, neroli and marjoram.
- Headaches and migraines improve with basil, chamomile, lavender, marjoram, peppermint and rosemary.
- Hyperventilation responds to fennel, frankincense and lavender.

From the listings of essential healing essences you can see that many ailments can be dealt with by just one or by several oils. This is another beneficial aspect of treatment with aromatherapy; chemical

drugs are designed to treat one or two ailments at one time, so if
many health problems are present, several pills and potions are
necessary.

The truly wonderful benefit of aromatherapy, however, is in its
healing effect not just on the body's systems, but on the emotions
and spirit also, which, when you are trying to break a dependency, is
invaluable.

Oils should be handled with care, as some can be potentially
dangerous in the hands of an inexperienced user. So for a serious
condition or a long-term disorder, a visit to an aromatherapist is to
be recommended. In any event, it is difficult to lie down and
massage oneself properly, even if the right blend and mixture of
essential oils has been selected.

Finding An Aromatherapist

For a list of practitioners or further information, please write,
enclosing a SAE to:

Aromatherapy Organisations Council, 3 Latymer Close,
Braybroke, Market Harborough, Leicestershire LE 16 8LN;

International Federation of Aromatherapists, Department of
Continuing Education, Royal Masonic Hospital, Ravenscourt Park,
London W6 OTN.

Further Reading

Aromatherapy: A Definitive Guide To Essential Oils by Lisa Chidell
   (Headway)
Aromatherapy – Massage With Essential Oils by Christine Wildwood
   (Element)
Aromatherapy by Daniele Ryman (Piatkus)
Aromatherapy: Headway Lifeguides by Denise Brown (Headway)
Massage: Headway Lifeguides by Denise Brown (Headway)
The Art of Aromatherapy by Robert Tisserand (C W Daniel)

8
ACUPUNCTURE, ACUPRESSURE, REFLEXOLOGY, COLOUR THERAPY AND HYPNOTHERAPY: POSSIBLE RELEASE

Acupuncture and acupressure are ancient healing methods which come from the East. Traditional Chinese medicine, of which acupuncture and acupressure are a part, is inherently linked to Chinese philosophy. This states that all living things are activated by a life force or energy called *chi*. Without *chi* there is no life. Traditional Chinese medicine is based on the idea that *chi* flows along particular channels in the body: these channels are called *meridians*. Treatment of an ailment according to Chinese principles is based on ensuring that the flow of *chi* is uninterrupted. The flow of *chi* is dependent upon the correct harmony of *yin* and *yang*. According to Chinese philosophy, all things in the universe have a *yin* and a *yang* aspect.

Yin And Yang

Yin and *yang* are two opposite but complementary parts: *yin* is traditionally associated with the qualities of movement, light, heat and vigour; in contrast *yang* with stillness, darkness, cold and inactivity. Neither can exist without the other: the ancient Chinese character of *yin-yang* is a mountain which has a shady aspect and a sunny aspect. So, without cold there is no heat, without light there is no darkness. Harmony is only possible when both aspects are

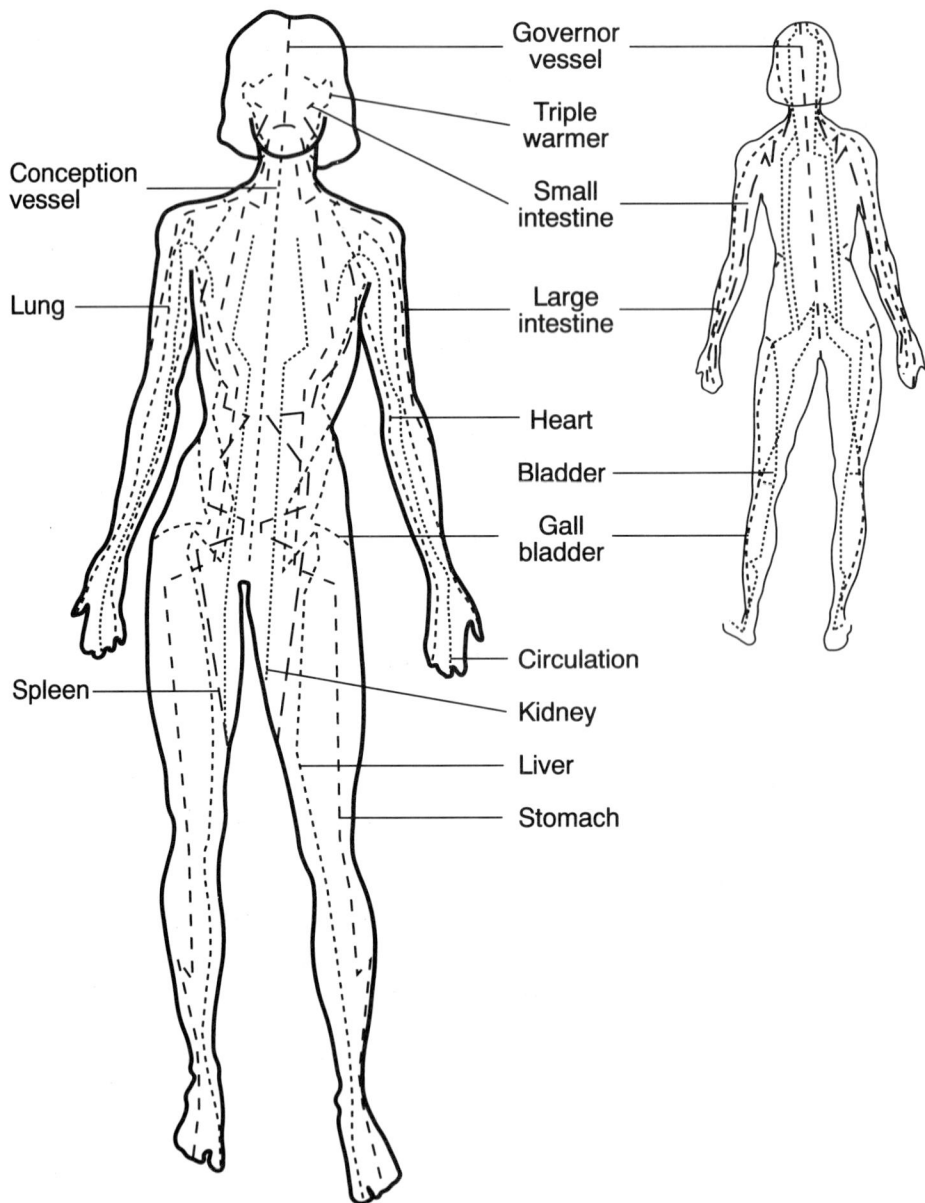

The meridians

present. *Yin* and *yang* control each other and *yin* and *yang* aspects can be further divided into *yin* and *yang*. If the body is unhealthy, it is because the *yin–yang* aspects are unbalanced. Chinese medicine therefore treats the body's energy equilibrium to restore and maintain good health. Acupuncture, acupressure and shiatsu are ways of entering the body's energy channels.

There are 12 major meridians. These meridians (except for the *triple warmer*) are named after the parts of the body to which they relate, that is, the *large intestine, stomach, heart, spleen, small intestine, bladder, circulation, kidney, gall bladder, lung* and *liver*. In addition there are the *central* and *governing* meridians. Manipulation of points along the particular meridians is said to influence the *chi* and *yin-yang* balance.

A body which is subject to an addiction is, as a result, out of kilter; its balance is upset and its harmony consequently lost. Chinese acupuncture would set about restoring the body's flow of energy and its balance: when these two are achieved, the need for the addiction and the addiction itself pass.

Acupuncture

How Does Acupuncture Work?

The body's energy network is tapped into by inserting various needles at strategic points below the skin. There are some 800 acupuncture points which link to the 12 major meridians. Scientific research has not found any evidence of the meridian channels, and this in our western world, amounts to possible condemnation of acupuncture as hogswash. Yet millions of people can testify to the very real effects of acupuncture – acupuncture is common medical practice in the East – so how does it work?

Aware that acupuncture is somehow effective, one theory is that acupuncture encourages the body to release natural painkillers, the *endorphins* and *enkephalins*. These painkillers are known to be effective in treating depression and allergies. The anaesthetising effect of acupuncture has also been attributed to the *gate control theory* (the theory that there are *neuropathways* to the brain via the spinal cord which, if blocked, cannot send messages of pain to the brain). While this may account for the anaesthetic effects of acupuncture, it does not explain acupuncture's success in healing non-painful conditions. In any event, acupuncture's ability to block

pain could be of immense benefit to addicts who are trying to
withdraw from their addictive substance.

A Visit To An Acupuncturist

Acupuncture is not a simple affair and a qualified acupuncturist has
taken years to master his or her skills. Recently the British Medical
Association has issued warnings against acupuncturists, but this
applies to cowboys who may only have taken a weekend course in
acupuncture to learn the rudimentary pain-killing methods. It is
consequently advisable to ensure that practitioners are suitably
qualified and experienced: there are four professional bodies which
are affiliated to the Council for Acupuncture which maintains a
register of practitioners (see 'Finding A Practitioner' at the end of
this chapter).

The professional acupuncturist will base diagnosis on several
factors. Pulse diagnosis involves readings of 12 different pulse beats
– six to each wrist – each corresponding to one of the 12 meridians.
There are 28 different qualities which can be recognised from the
pulses, from *weak* and *slow* to the less obvious *tight, hasty, thin* and
fine. A fairly detailed picture of the energy flow can be obtained
from the pulse readings.

Further diagnosis is based upon the appearance of the face, skin,
tongue (in itself a highly diagnostic tool), eyes, voice tone, gestures
and natural body odour. Some practitioners will also include
medical tests and a physical examination.

After the diagnosis is complete, the acupuncturist decides which
acupuncture points to manipulate for restoration of the patient's
energy pattern. Each point has a particular function attributed to it
and groups of points can act like a 'combination lock' whereby the
entire formula is more important than their relevant individual
attributes. The most usual way to do this is with fine needles,
usually made of stainless steel.

The Use Of Needles

Memories of painful injections or pinpricks do not enamour us to
the thought of having needles stuck into our body – we would have
to be pretty masochistic to be happy about that! Fortunately,
masochism is not one of the prerequisites of treatment by
acupuncture, since the actual procedure is relatively painless.

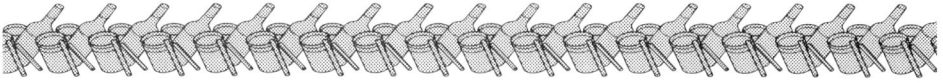

Insertion of the needles by a skilled practitioner feels a bit like a small pinprick, followed by a sensation of tingling, fullness or pressure. When correctly administered, no blood is drawn and the sensation may be felt up to a short time afterwards.

The needles themselves are very fine and are inserted vertically, obliquely or almost horizontally – usually only a fraction of an inch below the skin. Specialist treatment may call for different types of needle and deeper insertion may be required, although this is not considered to be any more painful than the lighter insertion.

Moxibustion is a type of acupuncture treatment involving a ball of dried mugwort or wormwood placed on top of the needle's handle; the needle is inserted and the herb set alight. Alternatively, the herb may be placed on the patient's skin, set alight and adroitly whisked away before any heat reaches the body. The needle is inserted afterwards.

Some practitioners pass an alternating electrical current down the needle in order to identify acupuncture points (points are identified by decreased electrical resistance). *Electroacupuncture* dispenses with needle insertion altogether and passes electrical current to the acupuncture points; this modern method is very popular.

Another form of acupuncture is *auriculotherapy,* which is based on the ear: 200 points on the ear have been charted with correlations to other parts of the body. Electronic instruments or needles stimulate the aural points and a 'press' may be left in the ear to continue its beneficial effect after the actual acupuncture session.

Acupressure

Acupressure is similar to acupuncture in that it uses the same points, but instead of using needles, it uses the techniques of massage.

When you have a headache and rub your temples you are employing acupressure to relieve the pain. Similarly, when you knock your elbow, for example, and rub it to ease the pain, that is also acupressure. Acupressure is the art of using the fingers to press particular points (the acupuncture points) on the body to stimulate the body's own healing powers. It can be practised anytime, anywhere and by yourself. The only equipment needed are your own two hands. The Chinese discovered the healing and health-maintaining effects of acupressure more than 5,000 years ago.

Tension, stress and insomnia are only some of the health problems which can be improved with acupressure, all of which are

pertinent when you are trying to come off an addictive substance. Anything which can make you feel calmer, in control and optimistic will strengthen your determination to stay off your addictive substance.

How It Works

Although there are various kinds of acupressure, all use the same pressure points, described as *potent points*. The potent points are the same as those identified in acupuncture, occurring on the 12 meridians through which *chi* passes. Stimulation of the potent points releases endorphins in the body, which blocks pain sensation and increases oxygen flow. This in turn relaxes the muscles and promotes healing.

The potent points tend to accumulate tension. Fatigue, stress, trauma and chemical imbalance prompt secretion of lactic acid. This in turn causes the muscles to contract and tense up. Pressure applied to a potent point stretches the muscle fibres; this improves blood circulation and enables the body to eliminate toxins. This is beneficial to the immune system and hence increases the body's resistance to illness.

Finding The Potent Points

There are three types of points: local, trigger and tonic:

- *Local point:* this is the actual place where pain is felt. Stimulation of a point in the same area as the pain itself brings relief.
- *Trigger point:* a local point can also trigger an effect in another part of the body which is on the same meridian.
- *Tonic point:* this is a point which maintains general good health. A popular tonic point is the webbing between the thumb and index finger.

The points each have two methods of identification. There is the original ancient Chinese name, which often describes the healing benefit. For example, *Shoulder Corner* describes the point to ease shoulder pain; *Three Mile Point* is so called because it apparently gives enough energy to run 3 miles! In addition, each point has a modern classification consisting of letters and numbers. This classification is universally used by professional practitioners both of acupressure and acupuncture. The points can be located by reference to anatomical pointers such as bones, joints and muscles.

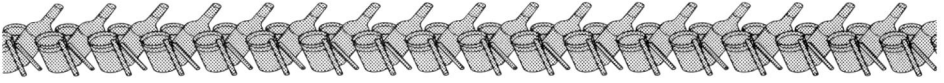

How To Practise Acupressure

There are four main types of pressure: firm, slow, brisk rubbing and quick tapping:

- **Firm pressure** is applied by thumbs, fingers, the palm of the hand and the knuckles. Areas of the body which have the more developed muscles, for example the shoulders and buttocks, need firm pressure. Pressure is applied for several minutes to relax an area or to relieve pain and for a few seconds if the intention is simply to stimulate circulation.
- **Slow**, kneading movements are used to loosen up stiff muscles.
- **Brisk rubbing** increases circulation, tones the skin and relieves chills and numbness.
- **Quick tapping** with the fingertips is for tender areas, such as the face, and improves nerve functioning.

Ideally, you should practise acupressure on a daily basis, for an hour at the most, but two or three times a week will also net benefits.

A Visit To An Acupressure Practitioner

You can practise acupressure, but a course with a practitioner could be helpful. Practitioners will usually use thumbs or fingertips to massage on the potent points, although elbows and even knees may be used. Sessions typically last between 30 and 60 minutes.

Reflexology

Reflexology is another ancient Chinese method of healing, although native American tribes and ancient Egyptians were also aware of its healing powers. Reflexology is based on the reflex areas of the foot which are massaged to bring benefit to other areas of the body. Sounds strange? If you have ever had your foot massaged, you will know that it is deeply satisfying and relaxes more than just the feet.

All Your Body Represented In Your Feet

Reflexologists consider that the whole body is represented in the shape and contours of the feet and that a map of the body could be drawn on the soles of the feet. The right foot represents the right side of the body and the left foot the left side. Terminal endings, or *pressure points,* are found mainly on the soles, but energy channels (*meridians*) can be stimulated or pressured at the sides and on the

tops of the feet and also up the sides of the ankles, where the
meridians enter or leave.

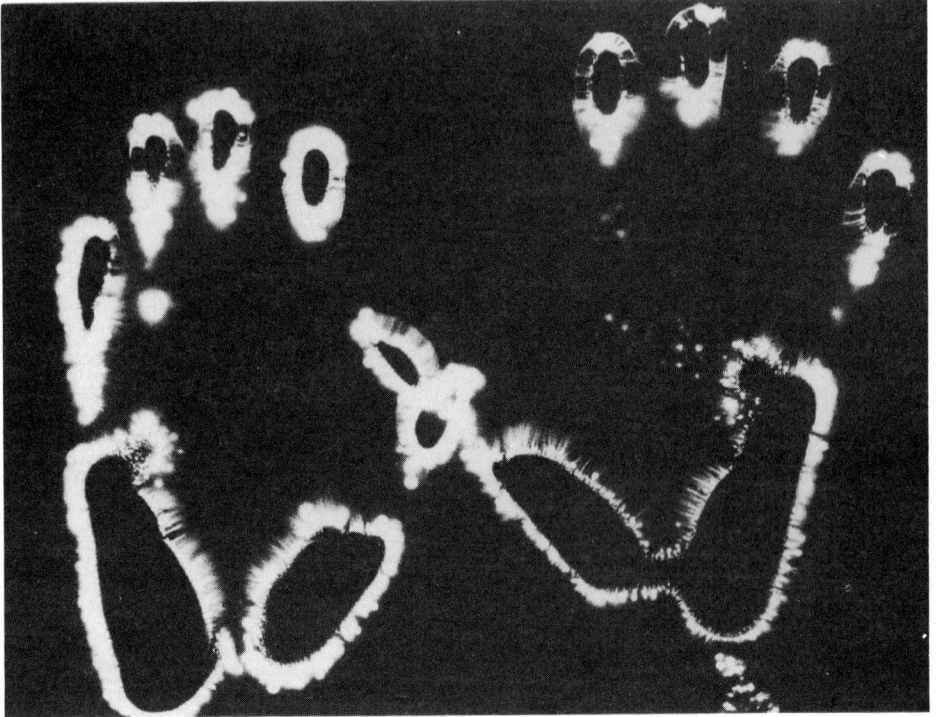

This Kirlian photograph of hands clearly shows the energy field which surrounds the body.

Kirlian photography is a special method of photography which
shows the energy fields of objects. Kirlian photographs have been
used to reveal a low energy in a certain part of the foot which
corresponds with a health problem in the body. After reflexology,
Kirlian photography shows an increase in energy in the pressure
point, suggesting that energy balance has been restored.

How Does Reflexology Work?

Reflexologists direct their treatments to the hands and feet of
clients, especially to the feet, which give the best response. The basis
of treatment is the belief that the body's energy flows through
energy channels, referred to as *meridians*. Meridians arise from all

organs and structures in the body, joining larger meridians at various energy centres, like the *ganlia* of the nervous system. Five major channels on either side of the midline collect all the flows, accumulating all sources before reaching the periphery in the hands and feet. The energy flows return inwards from the periphery, back to their sources, much like the circulatory system. Any blockage along the flow means that structures beyond the blockage are not at maximum efficiency and, if not already in disorder, will surely and eventually succumb to problems. Treatment is always of the whole, since the whole affects the part, and vice versa.

A Visit To A Reflexologist

Treatment will include counselling for lifestyle, diet and stress-promoting situations, as well as obtaining information about the client's medical history, to find out what has caused the imbalances to occur and, hopefully, to correct the problem or prevent recurrence. The first treatment is usually the most uncomfortable, as the deposits are concentrated in the periphery and need to be broken down. The discomfort becomes less with each subsequent treatment.

Colour Therapy

City dwellers, surrounded by tarmac roads, 24-hour shops and buildings of every description, go to great lengths to bring a reminder of the natural world into their city life. Modern man still needs to be in touch with nature, to see green trees and green grass. Paint manufacturers produce colour charts which explain that blue is 'relaxing', peach is 'warm', yellow is 'bright'. Interior designers use colour very carefully. It seems, then, that as human beings, we are responsive to colour and cannot exist happily in a grey world. Colour therapy takes this reaction to colour a stage further – to aid healing.

It is known that different colours emit different wavelength frequencies in the colour spectrum. Colour therapy uses the vibration of the wavelength to bring about different results. Ultrasound is used by conventional medicine to detect and to heal; colour therapy uses colour in the same way. Each body cell, organ, muscle and bone vibrates to a set frequency. If the frequency is incorrect, it can be corrected using colour.

Healing With Colour

Colour can be radiated: coloured gemstones and crystals simply held in the hand and meditated upon can be used to bring about the desired effects. A colour therapist will visualise colour and 'channel' it to the patient to effect healing. The patient will be expected to visualise the colour also, and to meditate on its attributed healing potency. It might be suggested that they start wearing clothes of that colour or they redecorate their rooms. If the patient is not sensitive to colour nor positive about its healing powers, the success of colour therapy is limited.

Hypnotherapy

Hypnotherapy can be a very useful therapeutic tool in the management of most addictions and can complement many of the therapies described earlier in this book. The myths and mystery surrounding the use of hypnosis should not deter you from its benefits. Fears of being controlled or manipulated, or even induced into a deep trance state are totally unjustified. Hypnotic subjects will not do or say anything that they do not want to. Under hypnosis, the experience of most people is that they are fully aware of what is going on and they are able to remember what has taken place after the session has ended.

Hypnosis can be described as being in a state of intense concentration accompanied by deep physical relaxation. It can be a very pleasant and relaxing experience. It is important to realise, however, that in itself, hypnosis cures nothing. It is the state of increased awareness and sensitivity which allows the cure to take place. Indeed the factor that will determine how effective hypnotherapy will be, is the patient's involvement in wanting to change addictive habits. It is the patient's motivation combined with constant involvement in the therapy that makes hypnotherapy a useful aid to shaking off addiction.

What does the hypnotherapist do?

Hypnosis usually follows a standard pattern. The therapist will talk in a slow, relaxing, controlled and confident way, drawing the patient's mind into a concentrated and detached state of relaxation. The hypnotherapist may suggest that the patient's body is becoming

heavier and more relaxed and the mind more tranquil and peaceful. Some therapists use visualisation and ask the patient to imagine lying on a white, sunny beach or perhaps taking a walk down a county lane; or the patient may be asked to concentrate on an object visually. The therapist then encourages heaviness and closing of eyes, followed by other simple test instructions, such as the raising of an arm. By this stage, the patient is usually in a light trance. Deeper levels are attained by the therapist counting from 1 to 10, or asking the patient to imagine descent in a lift, for example.

Once in this light trance, the patient may relax both mentally and physically. This is not too dissimilar to the period just before falling asleep. This state of relaxation can be used in different ways. With the conscious and analytical part of the mind relaxed, many hypnotherapists will use hypnosis to give suggestion therapy, (for example, the therapist may tell you that you do not need cigarettes, that you have no desire to drink or that you are happier without drugs). The session may last anything from 30 to 60 minutes. You are then brought back to full consciousness and you should feel pleasantly relaxed.

How long is the treatment?

At the initial consultation, which usually lasts about an hour, the therapist will discuss the course of treatment and explain exactly what the patient can hope to gain from the sessions. Some people need just one session to give up smoking while others may require many more. But patients can expect to become aware of positive progress after about four visits. It is also customary for a practitioner to teach a patient the technique of self-hypnosis to use after the condition, such as an addiction, has been brought under control.

Consulting a therapist

At the moment it is possible for anyone to set up as a hypnotherapist so it is important to check the credentials of any therapist you are considering consulting. Refer to the information at the end of this chapter on Finding A Practitioner to find a reputable hypnotherapist in your area.

Treating Addictions

Alcoholism

- Acupuncture is extremely successful in helping alcoholics to kick their habit, although it cannot cure alcoholism on its own. Counselling and psychotherapy will also be necessary. To minimise withdrawal symptoms, however, acupuncture can help – a daily treatment for the first 5 to 7 days, according to the withdrawal symptoms, is beneficial. Acupuncture points are likely to target the stomach, bladder, lung, spleen, kidney, circulation and the heart. Other points will be used to ease withdrawal symptoms, such as insomnia, loss of appetite, profuse sweating, extreme agitation, vomiting, exhaustion and headache.
- Acupressure would typically target the potent points of Joining the Valley (to relieve general pain), Heavenly Pillar (to relieve stress, exhaustion), Gates of Consciousness (to ease aches and pains, irritability), Abdominal Sorrow (for the digestive system), Bigger Rushing (for boosting morale), Wind Mansion (to ease head congestion, mental stress), Facial Beauty (for bloodshot or swollen eyes, head congestion) and Drilling Bamboo (relief of sinus pain, painful eyes).
- Reflexology would concentrate on the zones which relate to the liver, bladder, kidneys and head.
- Colour therapy would employ blue for the liver, to ease tension for headaches and insomnia, and turquoise for the bladder.

Caffeine

- Acupuncture would ease caffeine withdrawal by using the points relating to vomiting and nausea, exhaustion, headache, irritability and agitation.
- Acupressure would concentrate on stress reduction, frustration and irritability. Potent points include Shoulder Well, Centre of Power, Letting Go, Sea of Tranquillity and Jumping Circle.
- Reflexology would work on the areas associated with the stomach, fatigue and kidney problems and general stress reduction.
- Colour therapy would prescribe blue for tension and stress.

Heroin

- Acupuncture can treat the withdrawal symptoms of nausea, headache, exhaustion, vomiting diarrhoea, chills, photosensitivity, insomnia, palpitations, night sweats and sore throats by targeting the gall bladder, stomach, kidney, spleen, circulation, governor vessel, lung, heart, intestines and triple warmer.
- Acupressure is successful in easing nausea, pain (potent points: Joining the Valley, Third Eye Point), stomach aches (potent points: Sea of Vitality, Sea of Energy, Centre of Power) and boosting the immune system (potent points: Sea of Energy, Sea of Vitality, Elegant Mansion, Three Mile Point, Joining the Valley, Bigger Stream, Bigger Rushing).
- Reflexology would be helpful to the heroin addict by working on the areas of the digestive system, lungs, circulation, muscular tension and stress.
- Colour therapy: blue for muscular tension and stress, and to reduce pain; turquoise for general treatment of the lymphatic system.

Cocaine

- Acupuncture can treat withdrawal symptoms of nausea, headache, exhaustion, vomiting diarrhoea, chills, photosensitivity, insomnia, palpitations, night sweats and sore throats by targeting the gall bladder, stomach, kidney, spleen, circulation, governor vessel, lung, heart, intestines and triple warmer.
- Acupressure is successful in easing nausea, pain (potent points: Joining the Valley, Third Eye Point), stomach aches (potent points: Sea of Vitality, Sea of Energy, Centre of Power), relieving sinus problems (potent points: Drilling Bamboo, Heavenly Pillar, Penetrate Heaven, Welcoming Perfume, Facial Beauty, One Hundred Meeting Point, Middle of a Person, Joining the Valley) and boosting the immune system (potent points: Sea of Energy, Sea of Vitality, Elegant Mansion, Three Mile Point, Joining the Valley, Bigger Stream, Bigger Rushing).
- Reflexology: targeting the pituitary gland (to boost hormone production, metabolism, etc.), digestive system, lungs, circulation, muscular tension and stress.
- Colour therapy: blue to reduce pain and palpitations, and ease stress; green for the pituitary gland.

Nicotine

- Acupuncture has helped many people to give up smoking. Up to ten treatments over 3 or 4 weeks are usual. Body points are chosen to target symptoms of dizziness, restlessness, insomnia, indigestion, nausea, cough and a tight chest.
- Acupressure would focus on the potent points of Letting Go, Shoulder Well, Sea of Vitality, Bigger Rushing and Sea of Energy to combat fatigue, dizziness, confusion, nausea and headaches.
- Reflexology would target the lungs to eliminate toxins and give general stress relief.
- Colour therapy: blue for relaxation and relief from irritability.

Sugar

- Acupuncture can help improve overall circulation to improve the skin and reduce nervous exhaustion.
- Skin problems can be improved with acupressure (potent points: Sea of Vitality, Three Mile Point, Heavenly Pillar, Four Whites, Facial Beauty, Wind Screen, Heavenly Appearance, Third Eye Point); as can anxiety (potent points: Sea of Vitality, Womb and Vitals, Heavenly Pillar, Sea of Tranquillity, Inner Gate, Third Eye Point, Rushing Door, Mansion Cottage).
- Reflexology: focusing on the circulatory system, kidneys and, for women, the female reproductive organs.
- Colour therapy: green for the pituitary gland and turquoise for the kidneys.

Tranquillisers

- Acupuncture for nausea, headache, exhaustion, vomiting, diarrhoea, chills, photosensitivity, insomnia, palpitations, night sweats and sore throats by targeting the gall bladder, stomach, kidney, spleen, circulation, governor vessel, lung, heart, intestines and triple warmer.
- Acupressure is successful in easing nausea, pain (potent points: Joining the Valley, Third Eye Point), stomach aches (potent points: Sea of Vitality, Sea of Energy, Centre of Power) and boosting the immune system (potent points: Sea of Energy, Sea of Vitality, Elegant Mansion, Three Mile Point, Joining the Valley, Bigger Stream, Bigger Rushing).
- Muscular tension and stress can be eased by reflexology.
- Colour therapy: blue to relax.

Food Addictions

- Acupuncture: body points to ease irregular bowels, constipation, vomiting, irregular menstruation, fluid retention or frequency, agitation, abdominal distension.
- Acupressure: potent points might include Penetrate Heaven (relief of headaches), Joining the Valley (depression, constipation, balances the gastrointestinal system), Severe Mouth (clears the stomach).
- Reflexology: targeting the stomach and digestive system.
- Colour therapy: blue for relaxation, relief from tension and irritability.

Finding A Practitioner

Acupuncture and Acupressure
The fact that anyone can call themselves an acupuncturist makes it all the more important that you establish that the practitioner is properly trained. There are four professional bodies which are affiliated to the Council for Acupuncture, 38 Mount Pleasant, London WC1X OAP, which maintains a register of practitioners. They are the British Acupuncture Association and Register, the International Register of Oriental Medicine UK, the Register of Traditional Chinese Medicine and the Traditional Medicine Society.

Reflexology
The British Reflexology Association, 12 Pond Road, London SE3 9JL, maintains a register of members which is updated three times a year. Its official teaching body is the Bayley School of Reflexology.

Colour therapy
For information on using colour tharapy in conjunction with reflexology, telephone Pauline Wills on 081 204 7672, or for general information on colour therapy, telephone The Hygeia College of Colour Therapy on 045 3832150.

Hypnotherapy
For a list of practitioners in your area, write, enclosing a SAE to The British Hypnotherapy Association, 1 Wythburn Place, London W1H 5WL. Tel: 071 723 4443.

Further Reading

Acupuncture by Alexander Macdonald (George Allen & Unwin)
Acupressure: Headway Lifeguides by Eliana Harvey and Mary Jane Oatley (Headway)
Acupressure's Potent Points by Michael Reed Gach (Bantam Books)
Reflexology and Colour Therapy Workbook by Pauline Wills (Element)
Reflexology: Headway Lifeguides by Chris Stormer (Headway)
Visualisation: Headway Lifeguides by Pauline Wills (Headway)

9

CONCLUSION

Addictions often come about as a result of need, a need which is unfulfilled and which leaves a hollow emptiness. Whatever the actual addiction, be it to food, tranquillisers, alcohol or nicotine, the addiction may be a means of filling the emptiness and hopelessness of dissatisfaction. But since many people feel hopelessness, yet do not turn to addictive substances, what sets the dependent personality apart? A lack of self-worth? Self-dislike? The inability to face problems with courage and self-control?

Or could it be more to do with the liver? The liver is a major organ of the body, responsible for expelling toxins and producing nourishing bile: it is a giver of life. Many addictions, particularly alcoholism, hard drugs and food addictions, damage the liver. Many ancient systems of belief regard the liver as the seat of emotions, notably that of anger. Liver disorders are representative of anger towards ourselves and to others. If the liver cannot function to expel toxins, that is, anger, the body as a whole suffers and the cycle of self-destruction continues; a cycle which can only be broken when we learn to love ourselves unconditionally and face our problems, and therefore our addictions, with courage and determination.

Addictions are not simply a matter of a chemical dependence on a substance or of the related problems of a damaged immune system or liver: they are a classic example of a body–mind interaction. But then which disorder is not?

Does it make a difference which of the therapies, orthodox or complementary, you choose to attain health and well-being? There is no simple answer to this. If you are looking to eliminate the symptoms of your disorder as opposed to healing, then any therapy that quickly and effectively deals with the symptom would be acceptable. However, if you consider healing as attaining health and being wholly well again, then you have to look at all the therapies in a very different light.

When the body malfunctions, it has an effect on us at various levels. If I say I have a headache, it means that the pain which is manifesting itself in my head is in me as a person. If I just treat the head by, for example, taking aspirin, it means I am disregarding the source of inner pain.

Neither the GP and his drugs, nor the herbalist and her herbs, nor the aromatherapist and his essential oils, nor the acupuncturist and her needles, nor the osteopath and his manipulation, nor the anthroposophical doctor with her art therapy, eurythmy and hydrotherapy can heal. **Only you can heal yourself**. 'Each patient carries his own doctor inside him,' said Dr Albert Schweitzer. In order to begin the process of healing you must want to achieve health. The will to get better comes into play and mind–body interaction has to be acknowledged.

A cognisance of this body–mind interaction will result in an integration of the body and the mind in the process of achieving wellness. That is what healing is all about. If this is understood, then it is easy to understand why the therapies described in this book can be effective. Whatever therapy we may choose, it can only be effective if we have a positive attitude towards the healing technique and the person who helps us to heal ourselves.

The culture of dependency spawned by modern medical intervention, of curing the sick parts of the body, has conditioned us to lose faith in our own ability to heal ourselves. We have come to rely on medication as a form of reassurance and believe that the prescription will 'cure'. The root of this thinking is attributed to René Descartes whose dictum, 'I think therefore I am', crystallised the concept of separating *res cognitas* (the realm of the mind) and *res extensa* (the realm of matter). His perception of the material world has so permeated our culture that we now view the human body as an elaborate machine made up of assembled parts. Descartes said, 'I consider the human body as a machine. My thought compares the sick man and an ill-made clock with my idea of a healthy man and a well-made clock.' This legacy of dualism has guided and moulded the basis of modern medicine up to the present time.

Indeed, the study of disease has focused on biological processes, attributing the causes of all illness to biological factors. Modern medicine, preoccupied with measurements, statistical models and double-blind crossover studies fails to take into account the person as a whole and appears to preclude the human potential for self-healing. The mind–body relationship has been ignored in healing. Whatever the disease, unless we accept that this relationship does exist, it is not possible to achieve true healing or true health and well-being.

We must first recognise that mind and body are both aspects of

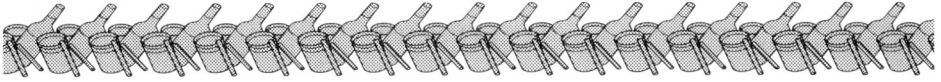

the human whole; that they are interrelated and cannot be seen in isolation from each other. The state of perfect balance between mind and body, as sometimes experienced in childhood, can be achieved.

We have seen that the immune system is indispensable for defence against disease-causing substances. However, we can be left vulnerable to disease if certain hormones are released by the adrenal glands which disrupt the relationship between the brain and the immune system. In addition to stress, this disruption can be caused by repressed feelings such as prolonged anger, bitterness and other negative emotions and thoughts.

The limbic system, a ring-shaped area in the brain, consists of clusters of nerve cells, including the hypothalamus. Called the 'seat of emotions', the limbic system regulates the autonomic nervous functions, such as sweating, digestion and heart rate, and has a bearing on our emotions and sense of smell. The limbic system is therefore important in the body–mind relationship. This, in turn, is influenced by the cerebral cortex (the part of the brain responsible for thinking, perception, memory and all other intellectual activity).

Stress is an example of the result of the alarm bells sounded by the cerebral cortex when it perceives a life-threatening situation. As soon as the alarm bells ring, the limbic system and consequently the nervous system and the immune system are all galvanised into action. The reaction is tense muscles, constricted blood vessels and other symptoms that set into motion a general nervous disarray.

Sometimes the reactions are instantaneous, such as blushing; others, such as repressed anger, are cumulative and take longer to manifest themselves in the form of disease.

There is little doubt that there is an innate link between the mind and the body, each affecting the other. Negative thoughts and emotions will result in weakened defences which will lead to disease and, ultimately, death. Our recognition of the body–mind connection is reflected in our everyday language when we say, 'he is eaten up with jealousy', or 'his heart is broken', or 'the stress is killing him', or 'he is worn down with grief', or 'she is radiantly happy'.

Most of the traditional healing disciplines, based on different world views and cosmological principles, all have a common thread: they deal with illness by considering human beings in the context of their relationship with the cosmos.

Traditionally, Muslim physicians like Avicenna regarded man as an organic whole, composed of body and mind and endowed with a purposeful life-force.

The Yogic view of the human body is that it is composed of three different manifestations, namely, the physical body (composed of flesh, blood and bone), the subtle body (containing the life force *prana*) and the spiritual body (which encompasses universal wisdom).

To the Hawaiians, health means energy. Good health is a state of *ehuehu* (abundant energy) and poor health is *pake* (weakness). Illness is caused by *mai* (tension) and healing is equated to the restoration of *lapau* (energy). Health therefore is 'a state of harmonious energy'. The American Indians consider that Earth Mother is a living organism, and that all creations on this earth contain a life force and are part of a harmonious whole. Illness occurs when this balance is upset and the purpose of healing ceremonies is to restore both personal and universal harmony.

Tai Chi is the Chinese way of increasing the energy flow in the body and strengthening the body's resistance to ward off disease. Tai Chi is thought to stimulate the kidney (seen as the life force energy) and to maintain vitality of mind, body and spirit.

Rudolf Steiner, the founder of anthroposophy (see Chapter 6), sought to go beyond the idea of healing the body. His acute perception led him to explore the spiritual side of existence which led to an understanding of the ways of stimulating the natural healing forces in the person. Healing was a matter of considering the interrelation between the four aspects of the human being (physical body, etheric body, astral body and the ego) and treating them as a whole.

There are striking similarities in the various healing systems reviewed above. Call it by any name – *prana, chi*, life force, *ehuehu*, etheric energy – we all have it in us . It is up to the 'doctor inside', to borrow Albert Schweitzer's phrase, to harness this healing force within us and so to achieve that state of balance between body, mind and spirit.

Of late, the holistic model of health care has begun to gain momentum. The proponents of this model have gone some way to counter some of the overly mechanistic and reductionist streaks in modern medicine, although this does not mean denying the undoubted achievements of science. Holism is based on the premise that the human organism is a multidimensional being, possessing body, mind and spirit, all inextricably linked and that disease results from an imbalance either from within or from an external force. The human body possesses a powerful capacity to heal itself by

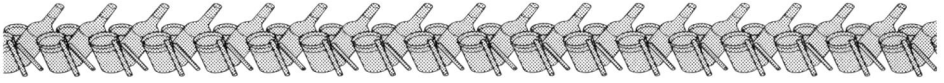

bringing itself back into a state of balance; the primary task of the practitioner is to encourage and assist the body in its attempts to restore this balance. Except in emergencies, the practitioner's role is that of an educator rather than as an interventionist.

The true test of healing must surely be a practical manifestation of harmony between the mind, the body and the spirit. Holism has some answers but matters of the spirit, while acknowledged, remain untouched and are even avoided in practice. Yet without the spiritual dimension no system of healing can be whole. There can be no true self-healing and no true holistic medicine unless the spirit is also recognised.

You picked up this book because you or a loved one suffers from dependency and because you have an open mind, you are willing to explore different types of interaction between the body and the mind. **You** are responsible for drawing spirit into the equation and the final message of this book is that so-called 'holism' that looks only at the mind and the body, ignoring the spirit is an illusion – go for a truer reality and use this book as, perhaps, a first step on the road to uniting body, mind and spirit.

GLOSSARY

Acute Symptom that comes on suddenly, usually for a short period.

Adrenaline Hormone released by the adrenal gland, triggered by fear or stress.

Allergy A condition caused by the reaction of the immune system to a specific substance.

Allopathy A term used to describe conventional drug-based medicine.

Amino acids A group of chemical compounds containing nitrogen that form the basic building blocks in the production of protein. Of the 22 known amino acids, 8 are considered essential because they cannot be made by the body and therefore must be obtained from the diet.

Anaemia A condition that results when there is a low level of red blood cells.

Analgesic A substance that relieves pain.

Antibiotic A medication that helps to treat infection caused by bacteria.

Antibody Protein molecule released by the body's immune system that neutralises or counteracts foreign organisms.

Antidote A substance that neutralises or counteracts the effects of a poison.

Antigen Any substance that can trigger the immune system to release an antibody to defend the body against infection and disease. When harmless substances like pollen are mistaken for harmful antigens by the immune system, allergy results.

Antihistamine A chemical that counteracts the effects of histamine, a chemical released during allergic reactions.

Antioxidants Substances which inhibit oxidation by destroying free radicals. Common antioxidants are vitamins A, C, E and the minerals selenium and zinc.

Antiseptic A preparation which has the ability to destroy undesirable micro-organisms.

Artherosclerosis A disorder caused when fats are deposited in the lining of the artery wall.

Atopy A predisposition to various allergic conditions like asthma, hay fever, urticaria and eczema.

Auto-immune disease A condition in which the immune system attacks the body's own tissue e.g. rheumatoid arthritis.

Benign Non-cancerous cells; not malignant.

Beta carotene A plant substance which can be converted into vitamin A.

Bile Liquid produced in the liver for fat digestion.

Candida albicans Yeast-like fungi found in the mucous membranes of the body.

Carcinogen Cancer-causing substance or agent.

Cartilage Connective tissue that forms part of the skeletal system, such as the joints.

Chi Chinese term for the energy that circulates through the meridians.

Cholesterol A fat compound, manufactured in the body, that facilitates the transportation of fat in the blood stream.

Chronic A disorder that persists for a long time; in contrast to acute.

Cirrhosis Liver disease caused by damage of the cells and internal scarring (*fibrosis*).

Collagen Main component of the connective tissue.

Constitutional treatment Treatment determined by an assessment of a person's physical, mental and emotional states.

Contagious A term referring to a disease that can be transferred from one person to another by direct contact.

Corticosteroid Drugs used to treat inflammation similar to corticosteroid hormones produced by the adrenal glands that control the body's use of nutrients and excretion of salts and water in urine.

Detoxification Treatment to eliminate or reduce poisonous substances *(toxins)* from the body.

Diuretic Substance that increases urine flow.

DNA A molecule carrying genetic information in most organisms.

Elimination diet A diet which eliminates allergic foods.

Endorphins Substances which have the property of suppressing pain. They are also involved in controlling the body's response to stress.

Enzyme A protein catalyst that speeds chemical reactions in the body.

Essential fatty acids Substances that cannot be made by the body and therefore need to be obtained from the diet.

Free radicals Highly unstable atom or group of atoms containing at least one unpaired electron.

Hepatic Pertaining to the liver.

Histamine A chemical released during an allergic reaction, responsible for redness and swelling that occur in inflammation.

Holistic medicine Any form of therapy aimed at treating the whole person – mind, body and spirit.

Lymphocyte A type of white blood cell found in lymph nodes. Some lymphocytes are important in the immune system.

Malignant A term that describes a condition that gets progressively worse, resulting in death.

Meridian Energy pathways that connect the acupuncture and acupressure points and the internal organs.

Mucous membrane Pink tissue that lines most cavities and tubes in the body, such as the mouth, nose etc.

Mucus The thick fluid secreted by the mucous membranes.

Neurotransmitter A chemical that transmits nerve impulses between nerve cells.

Oxidation Chemical process of combining with oxygen or of removing hydrogen.

Placebo A chemically inactive substance given instead of a drug, often used to compare the efficacy of medicines in clinical trials.

Potency A term used in homoeopathy to describe the number of times a substance has been diluted.

Prostaglandin Hormone-like compounds manufactured from essential fatty acids.

Sclerosis Process of hardening or scarring.

Stimulant A substance that increases energy.

Toxin A poisonous protein produced by disease-causing bacteria.

Vaccine A preparation given to induce immunity against a specific infectious disease.

Vitamin Essential nutrient that the body needs to act as a catalyst in normal processes of the body.

Withdrawal Termination of a habit-forming substance.

INDEX

THE NATURAL MEDICINES SOCIETY

The Natural Medicines Society is a registered charity representing the consumer voice for freedom of choice in medicine. The Society needs the support of every individual who uses natural medicines and who is concerned about their continued existence in order to achieve the necessary changes needed to accomplish their wider availability and acceptance within the NHS.

The Society's aims are to improve the standing and practice of natural medicine by encouraging education and research, and by co-operating with the government and the EC on their registration, safety and efficacy. A major drawback in this work has been that none of the Department of Health's licensing bodies has any experts from these systems of medicine sitting on their committees – this has meant that not one of the natural medicines assessed by them has been judged by anyone with an understanding of the therapy's practice. Since the formation of the Society, it has worked towards the establishment of expert representation on the committees appraising these medicines.

To fulfil these aims, the NMS formed the Medicines Advisory Research Committee in February 1988. Known as MARC, its members are doctors, practitioners, pharmacists and other experts in natural medicines. It is the members of MARC who undertake much of the necessary technical and legal work. They have discussed and submitted proposals to the Department of Health's Medicines Control Agency (MCA), on how the EC Directive for Homoeopathic Medicinal Products can be incorporated into the existing UK system, and how medicines outside the orthodox range can be fairly evaluated.

The EC Directive for Homoeopathic Medicinal Products was eventually passed as European law in September 1992, incorporating anthroposophical and biochemic medicines, as well as homoeopathic. With discussions regarding the implementation of

the Homoeopathic Directive now in progress, the MARC's work begins in earnest.

In July 1993, the MCA sent out their consultation paper regarding the implementation of the Directive, which incorporates many of the suggestions submitted by MARC. In it they propose to set up a committee of experts to advise on the registration of homoeopathic, anthroposophic and biochemic medicines. This is a major step forward for the Society, and homoeopathy in general.

With MARC members becoming increasingly involved in the legislative process of the implementation of the Directive, the Natural Medicines Society can now move forward from the short-term aim of protecting the availability of the medicines, to the longer-term aims of promoting and developing their usage and status by instigating and supporting research and education. The NMS has already sponsored some research – it is important to stress here that the Society does not endorse, support or condone animal experimentation – including an expedition to the rain forests in search of medicinal plants, supporting a cancer research project at the Royal London Homoeopathic Hospital and contributing to a methodology Research Fellowship. On the educational side, the Society has published two booklets, with several more planned and has co-sponsored a seminar for doctors and medical students.

The Natural Medicines Society depends upon its membership to continue this unique and important work – please add your support by joining us.

IF YOU ARE NOT ALREADY A MEMBER WHY NOT JOIN THE NATURAL MEDICINES SOCIETY?

(BLOCK CAPITALS PLEASE)

Mr/Mrs/Miss/Ms _____

Address _____

_____

Postcode _____   Tel. No. _____

There is no 'fixed' annual membership fee. Please indicate below the amount you wish to pay: minimum £5 (students and unwaged); European countries £15; non-EC £20.

£5 _____   £10 _____   £15 _____

N.B. Pay by Deed of Covenant and/or Direct Debit if you can—please ask for details.

Donations and offers of practical help are also always welcome to aid our fight to return natural medicines to the mainstream of medical practice.

I enclose a donation of £ _____

Please return this form with your remittance (cheques and PO's payable to The Natural Medicines Society), to:

**THE NMS MEMBERSHIP OFFICE,
EDITH LEWIS HOUSE,
ILKESTON,
DERBYS,
DE7 8EJ.**

(Registered charity no.327468)

You will receive your Membership Card, Member's Handbook, Quarterly Newsletter.

Author Profiles

Hasnain Walji is a writer and freelance journalist specialising in health, nutrition and complementary therapies, with a special interest in dietary supplementation. A contributor to several journals on environmental and Third World consumer issues, he was the founder and editor of *The Vitamin Connection – An International Journal of Nutrition, Health and Fitness,* published in the UK, Canada and Australia, focusing on the link between health and diet. He also launched Healthy Eating, a consumer magazine focusing on the concept of a well-balanced diet, and has written a script for a six-part television series, *The World of Vitamins,* shortly to be produced by a Danish Television company. His latest book, *The Vitamin Guide-Essential Nutrients for Healthy Living,* has just been published, and he is currently involved in developing NutriPlus™: a nutrition database and diet analysis programme for an American software development company.

Dr Andrea Kingston MB ChB, DRCOG, MRCGP, DCH is a Buckinghamshire GP in a five-doctor training practice who has for some years been interested in complementary approaches to healthcare as well as psychiatry and Neuro-linguistic Programming. Hypnotherapy is her major interest, and she has used this technique to help patients throughout the last eight years. As a company doctor to Volkswagen Audi, she contributes regular articles to the company magazine, *Link.* In the past, she has served as a member of the Family Practitioners Committee and as the President of the Milton Keynes Medical Society.

Books by the same authors in the Headway Healthwise series:
- Skin Conditions
- Asthma & Hay Fever
- Headaches & Migraine
- Heart Health
- Arthritis & Rheumatism